Philip Rigby

NOT IN
VAIN

NOT IN VAIN

The Story of North Africa Mission

FRANCIS R. STEELE

William Carey Library

1705 N. SIERRA BONITA AVE • PASADENA, CALIFORNIA 91104

Library of Congress Cataloging in Publication Data

Steele, Francis Rue, 1915-
   Not in Vain

   Includes index.
   1. North Africa Mission—History. I. Title
BV3510.74   266'.00961   81-6122
ISBN 0-87808-182-8   AACR2

Published by the William Carey Library
P.O. Box 128-C
Pasadena, California 91104
Telephone (213) 798-0819

PRINTED IN THE UNITED STATES OF AMERICA

CONTENTS

ILLUSTRATIONS

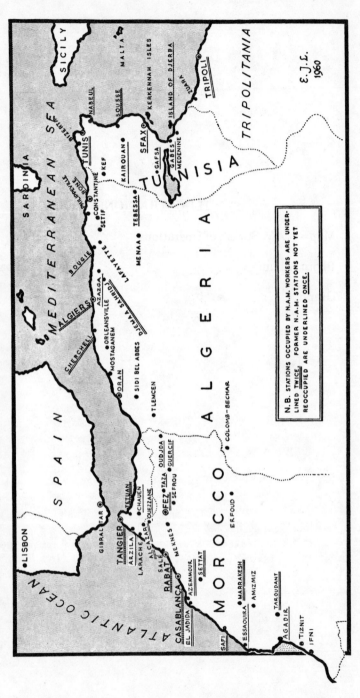

FOREWORD

I was relaxing alone in the livingroom of one of the old missionary furlough homes in Ventnor, New Jersey, while the children were getting reacquainted with the American way of life at the oceanfront. A knock came at the door. Who could it be? Although I felt sure that no one knew where we were, I opened the door to discover an old family friend, a veteran missionary from North Africa.

My mind filled with fresh memories of our first term of service in Japan. It had not been in vain; we had learned the language and established two vigorous churches. I was filled with the anticipation of a life of fruitfulness invested in Japan.

I asked my older brother about his ministry. "Robertson," he said, "if a missionary goes to a Muslim land with the anticipation of seeing people converted, one of two things will happen: he will change his expectation or he will leave."

Here before me stood a valiant warrior, bending over his cane, his health spent. I wondered how he could have invested half a lifetime in vain.

He seemed to sense the question in my mind and responded, "We stay there to vindicate the name of our God. That is the only motivation that will keep a missionary faithful and sane." Since that day I have thought much about the ministry of "vindicating the name of our God." Will it happen on the Day of Judgment when people who have heard and rejected the claims of Christ are without excuse because of the missionary's witness? In what way did this heroic remnant provide a vehicle for the Holy Spirit to convict the world of sin, or righteousness, and of judgment to come? The ministry of vindicating the name of God has not been in vain.

But is that all? No, a century's proclamation of the gospel has borne some fruit in North Africa. The firstfruits of the harvest have been gathered. Not in great numbers, perhaps, and not in every place. But over the years God has called Muslims to salvation.

In the eighties a fresh breeze of new expectancy is blowing. Hope has begun to stir that there is another way in which these long years of apparently fruitless ministry may prove not to have been in vain. Has it not been a time of plowing and sowing, preparing for a larger harvest in these last decades of the century?

One thing I learned well in our second term in Japan. He who expects no response will get exactly what he expects. While it may not be true that everyone who does expect a response will find it, certainly only those who expect a response are eligible to find it because this expectancy is another word for "faith." This new expectancy and this new faith can be seen especially in the North Africa Mission with its exciting plan to do something that has not been done in North Africa for fifteen centuries—establish twenty-five local congregations!

> Faith, mighty faith, the promise sees,
> And looks to God alone.
> Laughs at impossibilities,
> and cries, "It shall be done!"

One of the greatest friends of the Arab people, Dr. Francis Steele, has prepared for us in this centennial volume a fascinating backdrop for this great vision of faith. Indeed, the ministry of the past has not been in vain, nor will the ministry of the future be easy. But as we pass from the era of simply vindicating the name of our God, through courageous and faithful proclamation, to the era of expectancy born of faith, we will find that the witness has not been in vain.

Robertson McQuilkin, President
Columbia Bible College

PREFACE

A book which would put before the public some account of the countries of North Africa, their peoples and religion, together with an account of the objects and progress of the Mission, has long been needed. The difficulty was to find someone acquainted with the facts in question, and having sufficient leisure to write it. . . .

My work has been delayed by the constant pressure of Mission work both at home and abroad and by my lack of experience in a work of this sort. A few pages have been written, and then the work has been put aside for weeks and even months to meet pressing claims in other directions. . . . I must, therefore, beg that readers will make allowances for its many imperfections.

Thus wrote Mr. Glenny, one of the founders and long time Honorary Secretary of the NAM, in his preface to the book *The Gospel in North Africa* which he co-authored with Mr. Rutherford in 1900.

I know how he felt. For several years as our Centennial (read *Centenary for U.K.*) approached I have insisted that a record should be made of God's faithfulness to NAM over the years. A frequent rejoinder was, "It won't sell." Perhaps not. But my conviction was that if it were available those who wished would be able to find in its pages a condensed account of the rich heritage which is ours today, what brave and noble spirits have preceded us, and what a costly foundation has been laid in terms of lives sacrificed. It should inspire and encourage us today as we face our problems to know how God honored their faith.

Eventually, it was agreed that a book should be written and we began a search for a writer. All efforts failed; all invitations to write a history for us were politely declined. So we had a plan for a book and no author. Then it happened. As I might have suspected the official directive stated, "You wanted this book so badly; you write it." So I empathize with Mr. Glenny.

In searching the records I was struck by three elements in the history of NAM. First, there is the interlocking relations between the founders of the three British missions now merged. Second, there was the foresight of the leaders regarding an indigenous church and the constant striving to that end. Third, there was the rapid growth in early days and the high cost in lives laid down in service.

The three Missions, North Africa Mission, Algiers Mission Band, and Southern Morocco Mission, now merged into one family, were closely related at their beginnings. The founding members in each case were: Glenny, NAM: Trotter, AMB; and Anderson, SMM. It is fascinating to note the intertwined influences which gave rise to these Missions and the outstanding Christian leaders involved in the moving of the Holy Spirit upon their lives.

Edward Glenny of NAM was converted under the preaching of George Mueller of Bristol. Curious about markets in Algeria, he consulted with an old friend, Grattan Guinness, who told him to look up George Pearse, an old friend of his father, who had recently been in Algeria. Incidentally, Mrs. Pearse was converted under the preaching of Mr. Grattan Guinness in Paris in 1858.

Lilias Trotter was challenged spiritually by D. L. Moody and inspired for Algeria by Mr. Glenny at a YWCA conference in 1887. Applying to NAM, she was turned down because of a weak heart. So she started her own work (and lived on for forty years!).

John Anderson was converted during the Alexander Campaign of 1859 in Scotland. He was challenged by Glenny to send workers to Southern Morocco and was appointed Principal of the Bible Training Institute of Glasgow at the advice of D. L. Moody.

One tends to think today that general recognition that the ultimate goal of missions must be the emergence of indigenous churches is a new idea. I was surprised to find that goal expressed again and again. "We venture to suggest. . . that steps could be taken to place upon the shoulders of these . . . people the privilege and responsibility of forming an indigenous church, governed and propagated by themselves," says one writer around 1925. Plans and programs needed improvement but the vision was there.

Finally, the price paid during the early years was shockingly high. Few doctors and fewer hospitals were available; knowledge and treatment of disease was far inferior to those of today; transportation and communication were indifferent at best; the pages of the magazine are full of testimonials to the men and women who died in service on the field. What brave warriors!

I am sure you will understand that only a very small part of the record is contained in these pages. Selecting and condensing were necessary elements in the compiling of the account. I hope the thread of the story has not been lost and that the thrilling example of men and women trusting God shines through.

It is noteworthy, I think, that the majority of the older workers came from good Christian families and enjoyed the advantage of sound Christian training in church and home. Furthermore, they also seem to have engaged in considerable religious activity—Sunday school, evanglism, etc.—before offering for service with NAM. Then there followed the one year apprenticeship at Barking under Mr. Glenny's eagle eye. Mention should also be made of the outstanding caliber of men on the Council of the Mission in the early days, a firm foundation for the following years.

In an old book, *Daybreak in North Africa,* I found the following interesting note on the early occupation of Algeria by the French.

"In 1856 the French government conferred a great boon on the people of Algeria by boring for water in several places. A bountiful supply was procured by means of artesian wells, which seemed to the simple people quite miraculous. They named the first well 'Fountain of Peace,' the next they called 'Fountain of Blessing;' and the third 'Fountain of Gratitude.' " *Daybreak in North Africa,* p. 7 ff.

Twenty-five years later the "Fountain of Everlasting Life" was opened when the first missionaries arrived. May the years ahead witness the flourishing of the Church again in North Africa as patient, prayer-backed labor taps increasing sources of the Water of Life for North Africa.

ACKNOWLEDGMENTS

It is a pleasure to recognize and express appreciation for the persons and sources from which the material came which made possible the writing of this record. I was not able to engage in extensive research. Nor indeed was it necessary for a record of such concise dimension. In fact I had to condense my findings even further in order to keep within modest spacial bounds a story covering a hundred years.

There were two major published sources. First the official magazine of the Mission called *North Africa*. This periodical began with occasional papers (at a penny apiece) in 1884 and 1885. It became a quarterly in August 1885 and a monthly by 1890. In 1914 it fluctuated between monthly and bi-monthly but from 1915 continued as a bi-monthly down to 1938. Thereafter it was considerably reduced in size and content. But the earlier issues preserve an invaluable and helpfully detailed account of Mission affairs which delights the heart of the historian.

My second main source was the dissertation of Dr. Willy Heggoy entitled *Fifty Years of Evangelical Missionary Movement in North Africa*, 1881-1931 written for his Ph.D. at the Hartford Seminary Foundation in 1960. This book is a veritable gold mine of carefully researched and thoroughly documented information. If only someone had written a companion volume for the years 1931-1981 my job would have been virtually done for me.

The third major source of information was the official records of the North Africa Mission. Unfortunately, I did not have access to the British records. But actually a combination of the magazine *North Africa* with its detailed account down to 1940 on the one hand, and the records in our American office from 1948 on the other hand, substituted adequately for the absent earlier office documents from London and the nearly useless magazines from 1945 on, so that a reasonable account could be drafted.

I must also mention two small booklets on special subjects. *Set on a Hill*, by Dr. Farnham A. R. St. John and his sister, Patricia M. St. John, is a moving account of the Tulloch Memorial Hospital. And *No Frontiers*, by Jessie C. Stalley, tells the thrilling story of the growth of the Radio School of the Bible. Both were most helpful.

Mr. George McKenzie of the Southern Morocco Mission office in Glasgow provided me with some very helpful data about the early days of that Mission. And I got some very useful information about James Haldane from the tape of an address on Haldane by Rev. Gordon Fyles. I also benefited from interviews with several retired British missionaries. In particular, Mr. Harold Stalley shared impressions from his forty years of experience in North Africa, during most of which he served as the chief executive and field leader of NAM. Mrs. Cyril Morriss made an especially useful contribution which is contained in the "Helen Morriss" story of chapter three.

Several other persons have given advice and pointed out errors, which I have also appreciated. But the text is my own, and I accept full responsibility for it. It was my desire and aim to set forth the faithfulness of God in His direction of the NAM. Splendid men and women gave themselves to Him for His service. He did the work. If that comes through my efforts are amply repaid.

1

LAND OF THE VANISHED CHURCH

> We are of yesterday, and yet we have filled every place belonging to you, cities, islands, castles, towns, assemblies, your very camp, companies, palace, senate, forum. We leave you your temples only. Truth asks no favor for her cause. She knows that on earth she is a stranger, and that among aliens she may easily find foes. Her birth, her home, her hope are in the heavens. Nor does your cruelty profit you, though each act be more refined than the last. We grow up in greater number as often as we are cut down by you. The blood of the Christian is seed.
>
> Tertullian II Cent..

"IN DUE SEASON"

When we look back on a century of Gospel ministry in North Africa one major question presents itself: why is there so little to show for all the effort? In fact, the implications of such a question give rise to a second; was it worth while?

In facing such questions we must not forget that apparent results are not the sole criterion for determining success. Often statistics are inflated or converts do not persist. However, no intelligent Christian is unconcerned about results. Nor, on the other hand, will he allow paucity of response to discourage the expectation of any permanent results.

1

As we assess the evangelization of North Africa we must
recognize, first of all, a long period of neglect. The Barbary
States are within sight of continental Europe, have always been
involved in the political and economic struggles of Europe, and
therefore were both known by and accessible to European
Christians. Still, it was not until one hundred years after the
start of the modern mission movement that the first Protestant
missionaries made a concerted effort to reach North Africa.

Furthermore, since it is unlikely that, until relatively recently, many missionaries anywhere, even those working in highly
responsive areas, were actually trying to establish what would
be a truly independent national church in spite of vague claims
regarding indigenous principles it is not surprising that in
difficult and largely resistant countries missionaries tended to
settle for simple programs of itinerant evangelism and institutional work. Nevertheless, even under these circumstances,
wherever the Word of God has been proclaimed faithfully we
have the assurance of God's promise that it will not "return
unto Him void." There is no doubt whatever that thousands of
Muslims have been saved over the years by the faithful, brave
and often costly witness of missionaries.

So, then, we view the labors of the past as in themselves
eminently worth while and preparatory for the present. Gospel
literature has been dispersed widely and many thousands of
people today have some acquaintance with Christian truth. As
the political and social climate in North Africa has altered—
from largely isolated and religiously Muslim through a period
of European dominance to independent Muslim governments
fully aware of and active in world affairs—the plans and
programs of the Mission have matured to meet the current
situation. Rather than scattering personnel thinly and widely
as in the past, today we place groups in strategic areas—chiefly
metropolitan centers—where they can share their talents in
reaching students, business and professional people. Moreover,
every activity now is geared toward the development of the
National Church.

There is much that can be learned from the past. Great
servants of God blazed glorious trails of faith. And many laid
down their lives. There are abundant evidences of the extra-

ordinary leading and provision of God from the beginning through two World Wars, a world-wide depression, and the birth pangs of national independence. We have a noble heritage from the past and a bright prospect for the future. The example of their vision in the difficult pioneer days, the recent emergence of national Christian leaders, the growing concern and support of the Churches at home, all these encourage us to believe that there are even greater days ahead for the church of Jesus Christ in North Africa. Our confidence is in God. We believe that His plan will continue to materialize as we accept by faith the challenge before us. "In due season we shall reap if we faint not."

LAND AND PEOPLE

The countries of North Africa are bounded by sea and desert. The vast Sahara cuts them off from the rest of the African continent. Since bodies of water, even as large as the Mediterranean, constitute focal points for cultural development rather than dividing lines between cultures, it is no wonder that northern Africa has stronger affinities with the historical development of southern Europe than with the rest of the African continent to the south. In fact, the climate and ecology of the whole western Mediterranean basin is more or less uniform and therefore conducive to the development of similar agriculture and industry.

The geographical pattern of North Africa is made up of two parallel areas divided laterally by the great Atlas range of mountains. This mountain chain is intersected now and again by high plateaus of great productivity for cereal culture. The valleys intersecting the plateaus provide rich grazing lands. Further south the plain becomes ever drier through lack of rain until the desert proper is reached. Along the coast stretches a fertile plain which is rich in general agriculture: citrus and palm, vine and olive and garden crops of many kinds. Today this whole region is much less fertile and productive than in the past when thick forest covered the hills and many kinds of wild animals flourished in profusion. A continuing northerly shift in wind patterns over the centuries bringing less and less moisture from the sea has drastically changed the fertility of the plateaus and plains south of the Atlas. Then, too, overgrazing the land and stripping the forests has accelerated the desiccation. However, in spite of radical differences between the northern and southern sections of the African continent, it is the northern region rather than the southern which is properly designated "Africa" because that name was derived from a native Berber tribe which in Roman times lived in the area which is today called Tunisia. It seems that the name of these Berbers, the Aourigha, was later reduced by the Romans to a Latin form Africa. So, then, the first real Africans were people of Mediterranean racial type like the present inhabitants of Spain, southern France and southern Italy, not negroid at all; and they lived on the northern coast of the continent above the Sahara. Even the present separate countries of Morocco, Algeria, Tunisia, and Libya are not divided by well-defined physical or geographical boundaries. The whole region has always been essentially homogeneous with its original inhabitants speaking dialects of one common language, Berber. The political divisions came later.

The first significant group of foreigners to arrive on the shores of North Africa were the Phoenician merchants who sailed westward through the Mediterranean building trading and supply posts all along the northern coast of Africa and even some distance down the Atlantic coast as well. Eventually, a strong Phoenician base was established near the modern city of Tunis. It was called Kirjath Hadeshath (the "new city") in the Phoenician language as it was the capital of a newly established Phoenician colony. The name later assumed a Latinized form, Carthage, which it bore for centuries thereafter. From this base a powerful political and military empire grew until it threatened Rome for control of the Mediterranean basin. After a long period of conflict Rome finally defeated the Punic armies in 146 B. C., imposed a staggering war indemnity and destroyed the capital city of Carthage. However, about a century later, Julius Caesar rebuilt Carthage as the Roman capital of the Province of Africa and initiated the development of the territory as an important agricultural section of the Empire.

It was in the Roman period that Christianity was introduced

to North Africa and there grew from that seed a large, strong Church which provided some of the greatest theologians and leaders of the Christian world for centuries. Among these Churchmen was Tertullian the great apologist for the faith and defender against heresy who also in his writings established much, if not most, of the Latin vocabulary of Christian theology. The greatest leader of all, however, was Augustine, a Berber from what is now Algeria, who stands out as the supreme theologian of the early Roman Church. It is important to note that the early church in North Africa was from its inception exposed to bitter persecution from a hostile Roman government and many brave martyrs sealed their personal testimony to their faith in Christ with their lifeblood. Finally, in 313 A. D., the Emperor Constantine declared Christianity a legal religion of the Empire. Persecution virtually ceased; and compromise began.

In view of the strength and size of this early African Church whose magnificent ruins are still to be seen in eastern Algeria, Tunisia and western Libya it seems strange that it died out completely leaving no modern survival whatever in contrast, for example, to the surviving Coptic church in Egypt. Investigation of this question reveals facts of great importance to the work of Christian missions in North Africa today. There are two main reasons for the disappearance of that church. First, the Scriptures were never translated into the language of the native population. In fact, it was not until just after 1900 that the Bible was first translated into a Berber language when Mr. Cuendet completed his translation into Kabyle, a Berber dialect of present day Algeria. Therefore, secondly, Christianity never penetrated the native culture to any great depth. So as subsequent invaders arrived and attacked the so-called Roman Christian culture, the native peoples were either neutral or even sometimes actually supported the invaders against their own government which they felt was hostile to them.

There followed in succession the invasion of heretical Arian Vandals whose influence was largely destructive of both buildings and doctrine (thus the derivation of the modern word "vandalism" to refer to wanton destruction of property); the rescue from the Vandal heresy by Byzantine armies from

Constantinople who, unfortunately, brought with them the smothering weight of theological bureaucracy and exorbitant taxation; and finally the invasion of Muslim armies from Egypt. The Arab armies arrived around 650 A. D., swept westward as an irresistable stream, bypassing strong centers of Christianity in the large cities, until they reached the Atlantic coast then turned north to engulf Spain and cross the Pyrenees into France. This Islamic tide was only halted by the armies of Charles Martel at the battle of Tours in 732; just one hundred years after the death of the Prophet Muhammad. Centuries later the last Muslim ruler in Spain was driven out (1492) and the defeated Muslims flooded into Morocco.

There was virtually unending conflict between the Muslim invaders from the east and the local population. But eventually the organized Muslim governments were able to subdue the scattered Berber tribes. From time to time the Muslim rulers in North Africa cut themselves loose from the eastern Caliphate and developed powerful local dynasties. This was especially true of Morocco where a dynasty called the Alides still rules today in the person of King Hassan II.

However, the Berber people never capitulated readily to foreign rule of any kind. By and large they did assimilate Islamic culture blending with it some of their peculiar elements of lifestyle and religious animism so that North African Islam differs somewhat from its Near Eastern counterparts. In fact, the Berbers, a hardy, vigorous people, have always been a problem to every foreign invader from Phoenician to French. Never docile, with a strongly developed sense of independence, they were hindered in their defense of their land chiefly by their own separate tribal loyalties and lack of any unifying political element which could have made for an effective resistance to invasion.

In the sixteenth century Turkish political and military control was imposed on all of North Africa except Morocco which, due to strong local dynasties, was able to remain independent. Here again, though, the Turks as outsiders only really controlled the coastal areas and the larger cities with sporadic and largely unsuccessful attempts to extend their power more widely. During this period piracy developed as the growing maritime trade in the Mediterranean presented a strong and irresistible temptation for easy revenue by preying on foreign shipping and either selling captives into slavery or extracting heavy tribute for their ransom.

. As European interest grew from the end of the eighteenth century into the nineteenth, various powers involved themselves in efforts to stem piracy and stimulate trade. Spain, Portugal, France, Germany, Italy and England all vied with one another for favorable status until eventually, as a result of bargaining and treaty agreements, as well as overt acts of forceful intervention and capture, the French gained control of Algeria in 1830 and ultimately made it a Department of France. Tunisia became a French protectorate in 1883 after French troops invaded from Algeria. Tunisia's fall to European control resulted more from financial problems than an inability to exercise internal control and maintain peace. When the lucrative practice of piracy ceased following the intervention of European and American naval forces, there was simply no other adequate source of revenue. No money; no energy for government. As the European powers vied with each other for the privilege of "helping out," France won out by clever bargaining with the others and moved into control in 1881. Two years later Tunisia was a French protectorate. Morocco, likewise, with the exception of some territories in the North which were claimed by Spain, came under French control in 1912 after a series of expeditions by various European countries to preserve trading privileges and protect private citizens had failed. Basically good relations between France and Morocco resulted and thousands of Moroccans served in the French army in World War I. However, sporadic fighting continued with recalcitrant elements in the hinterland until 1934 when Morocco appeared finally pacified. In 1911 Italy moved into Libya—chiefly Tripolitania—both to regularize relations between the Pasha and Italian economic interest as well as to implement the settling of Italian colonists to relieve the pressure of over-population at home.

So all of North Africa found itself under European control. And thus things remained until aspirations for independence, which already existed in germinal form, grew in strength to

produce from the fires of revolution four independent countries
of basically Arabic culture and avowedly Islamic allegiance.
Libya was the first. Italy as a conquered nation after World
War II lost control of her colony. The world climate was not
conducive to European colonial acquisitions in 1947. So a
constitutional monarchy under King Idris was officially recognized in December of 1951 by the United Nations. This government was overthrown by a military junta under Col. Muammar
Qaddafi in 1969.

Independence movements had been spreading widely in the
other three countries though strongly opposed by the French
government. Tunisia took the first steps in negotiations
between its Neo-Destour party led by Habib Bourguiba (later
to become first President of independent Tunisia) and French
representatives. After months of bargaining, autonomy was
granted in 1955. Later, after Morocco had won full independence, Tunisia followed suit in March 1956.

The smoldering embers of independence in Morocco burst
into flame when Tunisia was granted limited autonomy. Violent
activity broke out everywhere; especially among Berber tribes.
In an attempt to halt further developments the French deposed
and exiled Sultan Muhammad V and replaced him with a servile
Berber puppet from southern Morocco. This act set off waves of
local violence countered by violent colonial reaction and blood-
shed. The impasse broke when a new French Resident General
took office who was sympathetic to the Moroccan cause. Still,
conditions worsened until France, convinced of its error,
restored the Sultan. Muhammad V skillfully negotiated the
final agreement and Morocco became a constitutional monarchy in 1956.

But the agony of Algerian independence was by far the
costliest and most painful of all. In the first place, France had
no intention whatever of giving up Algeria under any conditions. It was considered as an integral part of France, not a
colony. Therefore, there were fewer Algerians trained for
government and less local political cohesion for the pursuit of
independence. These two factors made for a long, painful period
of gestation. In 1958 discontent in France with the conduct of
affairs in Algeria reached such a pitch it brought down the IVth

Republic and General DeGaulle took charge. Now the tide of events changed and four years later after much talk and more suffering Algeria gained her long-sought independence. Not, however, before Algerian Muslims had displayed magnificent courage and restraint in the face of mindless butchery meted out in the final months by the Secret Army Organization, a cadre of die-hard French Military.

Now, one hundred and fifty years after the capture of Algiers in 1830, North Africa is again both politically and religiously Muslim and independent. That such a development might take place never occurred to Christian leaders of the Western World who during World War I anticipated the overthrow of the Ottoman Empire as opening a new day of unprecedented opportunity for Christian witness in Muslim countries. It is fascinating to read of the unjustified optimism expressed even by such great mission statesmen as Samuel Zwemer that when Muslim countries liberated from Turkish domination came under the control of the great "Christian" nations of Europe, England, The Netherlands and even France, the spread of the Gospel and the growth of the Church would be rapidly accelerated. Never again, it was thought would missionaries in Muslim lands be faced with the stern, unyielding opposition of Islamic leaders and teachers.

This enthusiastic optimism was doomed to disappointment on two grounds. First, the so called Christian nations did little to support Christian missions. More often than not, they signed treaties with the local Muslim authorities either strictly limiting missionary work or prohibiting it altogether. (France did tend to favor the programs of the Roman Catholic Church but always at the expense of Protestant organizations.) Second, the unexpected took place; the spirit of world-wide anti-colonialism and independence has restored Islamic control in the erstwhile Muslim colonies. Our dealings as a Mission now are no longer with European colonial authorities but with national Muslim leaders. One result of this is that virtually all foreign religious organizations have lost their legal status and have had to move administrative offices out of the North African countries; with the rare exception of those functioning in behalf of foreigners only. Another result is that we cannot obtain visas for our

personnel as missionaries. To some people these factors mean
that the North African countries are closed to missionary
activity. And in terms of the general practice of missions in the
past this is probably true. However, there is no reason why this
situation need necessarily mean that there is no way to
maintain a successful Christian witness. It simply means that
new methods must be formed which will permit a continuation
of the Gospel ministry so that the Church will grow again in
North Africa, the "land of the vanished Church."

CHRISTIAN MARTYRS OF THE PAST

In the long course of history since first the Gospel message
reached the shores of North Africa there have been many
occasions when courageous servants of God have refused to
silence or compromise their witness at the command of local
authorities and therefore have paid with their lives the price of
their loyalty. From that long stretch of time from the birth of
the Church in North Africa around 100 A. D. to the first arrival
of European missionaries in 1880 three examples have been
chosen to represent the unsung bravery of their colleagues. The
first, Perpetua, comes from the days of early Roman persecution. The second, Raymond Lull, represents the unique example
of a solitary witness to the love of Christ who went alone with
the Gospel rather than accompanying the explorers and ex-
ploiters of Catholic European countries which was the usual
practice of the medieval church. The third, Geronimo, is an
isolated exemplar of a national Christian in the face of Turkish
persecution.

Perpetua, 202
Born to a wealthy, patrician family in Carthage, Perpetua,
young mother twenty-two years of age, was imprisoned under
the edict of Septimius Severus in 202 A. D. She refused to offer
sacrifices to the heathen gods, stoutly maintaining her profession of faith in Christ her Savior despite agonizing pleas by her
distraught pagan father.
Finally, the day came. It was on the Emperor's birthday that

the Christians were to be killed by wild beasts in the Amphitheater at Carthage. The day before they all celebrated the
Agape feast with prayers and hymns. Then they marched into
the Amphitheater the next day to seal their testimony to faith
in God by their life's blood.

Many others thus bravely died maintaining by their courage
witness to the Gospel of God which later led to the founding of
the great North African Church.

Raymond Lull, 1315

Two drastically contrasting figures emerge from Europe onto
the stage of North Africa in the 13th century: Louis IX, King of
France, and Raymond Lull of Majorca, one a crusader of the
Cross, the other a crusader for the Christ.

King Louis IX led the Eighth Crusade and landed on the
ruins of Carthage in 1270 intending to recapture this territory
for the Church. In five weeks his army was decimated by the
plague and he himself lay dead; "not by might or by power..."

Twenty-one years later Raymond Lull sailed alone for Tunis
and entered it in the shining armor of the evangelist. A brilliant
scholar from a prominent family converted late in life, Lull developed a consuming passion for the Muslims of North Africa.
Learned in Scripture and Arabic, he set out at 56 years of age to
do what he could not persuade popes or priests to do; take the
Gospel to the Land of the Vanished Church. For years he debat-
ed with the Muslim teachers and slowly gathered together a
band of believers. Expelled from Tunis, several years later he
returned secretly to Bougie where he witnessed secretly for a
year gathering around him a little group of believers. Finally,
however, he spoke out in public denouncing Islam and was
stoned to death in 1315 at seventy-nine years of age. He stands
out as a lone beacon of Christian concern for Islamic North
Africa, or for missions anywhere for that matter, during a
period of centuries of neglect on the part of the Church. It was
almost six hundred years before an effective attempt to rebuild
the Church in North Africa began. ". . . but by my Spirit, say-
eth the Lord."

Geronimo, 1569

As a boy, Geronimo, an Arab, was captured by Spaniards and sold to a Spanish priest. Later he was restored to his parents. But at 25 years of age he returned to Oran to follow his Christian faith. During an attack on an Arab village, he was taken as part of the spoil and found himself a prisoner of the Turkish governor of Algiers. Vain attempts were made to turn him from his new faith. Eventually he was condemned to a most cruel death in 1569.

At a fort being constructed at Bab el Oued in Algiers, blocks of concrete were made on the spot in cases of wood. Geronimo, refusing to renounce his faith, was thrown bound hand and foot into the liquid concrete. In 1830 when the French took Algiers they tore the fort down. Workmen found a hollow place in one of the concrete blocks and poured in plaster of Paris making a cast of the body of Geronimo which can now be seen in a museum in Algiers.

When he heard of his impending death, he said, "Let not these despicable men think that they can frighten me by the thought of this death, or make me abandon the Christian faith."

2

BEGINNINGS:
1881—1931

"WHO WILL GO?"

The more we learn of North Africa and its inhabitants the more we feel the pressing need of more laborers. . . . What are we to do? Shall we obey the Lord's command and go, or leave them to perish in their sins? This is a personal matter, let each one ask of the Lord, "What wilt thou have me to do?"

Those who go . . . should not be novices, for the work needs much grace and wisdom . . . they should be first-class men, such as people say *can't be spared* from home. . . . Are there not some who will offer their services for these new Fields?

Edward Glenny
North Africa, Dec. 1884

"THRUST FORTH"

"Thrust forth"—from dear familiar friends and places
"Thrust forth"—to strange dark days, mid savage races
"Thrust forth"—to face and fight satanic forces
"Thrust forth"—to bear hard burdens, heavy losses.

"Thrust forth"—For lo! the Hand He strongly laid
upon your shoulder had to be obeyed
Because its pressure left, where it had lain,
The deep impress of nail-prints clear and plain.

"Thrust forth"—yet He Himself hath blazed ahead
And beaten out the track you are to tread
Then turning, He with out-stretched hand will meet you
His own "All Hail," in salutation, greet you.

"Thrust forth"—oh happy lot, oh glorious gain!
O'erwhelmingly worthwhile, the loss, the pain
To safeguard His redemption rights, and stand
Four-square for Him, in dark and distant lands.
Francis Augustus Rayner M.A.

Frank Rayner went out to Rabat, Morocco at the age of 31 in 1928. Graduated from Cambridge University he served as Classical Master at King Edward's School until his wife's death. Long a keen Christian with much experience in Christian service he had been burdened for foreign missions ever since his conversion at age fifteen. I found this poem in his handwriting in the mission house at Rabat on a recent visit.

THREE FOUNDERS

The North Africa Mission is a product of the Great Awakening or Evangelical Revival which began in Great Britain in 1859. A few years later great evangelistic campaigns like those of Moody and Sankey continued the work of the Holy Spirit among the people of England. Thus did God prepare Britain to launch missionary work around the world.

Three outstanding men of God, products of this period, were joined together in a marvelous way by the leading of God to bring about the founding of the North Africa Mission. Each one from his peculiar background and experience made his own distinct contribution and so, in November 1881, the first station of the North Africa Mission was established. The three men were George Pearse, H. Grattan Guinness and Edward H. Glenny. They were respectively an initiator, an encourager, and a developer. The unique personalities of these men and the way in which God prepared them and then brought them together so that each making his own contribution led to the foundation of NAM is a testimony to the wisdom of God in preparing special instruments in order to accomplish a specific task.

Mr. George Pearse had an unusual ministry. He seemed to have a special genius for exploring pioneer areas, launching some type of Gospel work there and then turning it over to others to continue. He was primarily an initiator. But he always seemed to find qualified associates to carry on.

Not much is known of his early life. He seemed to have overcome some skeptical ideas about Christianity as a youth and was converted in his mid teens. He entered business as a stockbroker and was so successful that in later years he was able to earn his living by three months work each year, spending the rest of the time in the Lord's service. He retired at age fifty-five. After the death of his first wife, he married Miss Jane Bonnycastle who had been converted under the ministry of Dr. H. Grattan Guinness in Paris in 1858.

Mr. Pearse's interest in the development of evangelistic works brought him in contact with many Christian leaders in Britain. He was a founding member of the Chinese Evangelization Society in 1850. Three years later this society sent out J. Hudson Taylor to China. Though the society itself collapsed shortly thereafter and Hudson Taylor later founded the China Inland Mission in 1865, the two men remained fast friends thereafter.

One of Mr. Pearse's greatest desires was to reach French soldiers with the Gospel. For that purpose he traveled frequently to France and started a Bible depot in Paris. However when clerical opposition made witness to the soldiers in France

virtually impossible, in 1876 the Pearses went to Algeria
seeking a ministry to French soldiers there, During their stay in
Algiers they had their first glimpse of the Kabyles from the
windows of their hotel, which overlooked an open space where
many of them used to congregate. The sight of these fine-
looking mountaineers awakened the sympathies of hearts accustomed to seek the salvation of souls, and suggested the
thought that something must be done to bring to them the light
of life and salvation. An incident which occurred served to
deepen this impression. There had been a time of famine,
followed by a terrible epidemic. Looking out from the window
one bright moonlight night, Mrs. Pearse saw what at first she
thought was a bundle of rags on a pavement under a wall, but
which, on looking more narrowly, she saw was a man. Another
lay near him, his ghastly face upturned to the moon. She could
not go out to help them, it was two o'clock in the morning, and
the house was locked up; she could only pray that help might
come to them. In the morning at six, when the Arab water-
carrier came, Mrs. Pearse asked him about those poor men.
They were dead, unpitied, uncared for. Seeing her emotion, the
man said, "Their fate affects me about as much as a dead dog
would; I am used to it; hundreds have gone in a short time."
The pitiful sight was graven upon Mrs. Pearse's mind, and the
spiritual condition of these people presented itself very vividly
to her—so neglected, so forgotten. It stirred her to earnest
prayer, and she and her husband never rested till something
was done to carry the Gospel to them.

Returning to London Mr. Pearse consulted with his friends
Dr. and Mrs. H. Grattan Guinness. Dr. Guinness urged him to
consider starting some work among the Muslim population of
Algeria and made a gift of one hundred pounds—the first gift
ever for the Mission which was later known as the North Africa
Mission.

In 1880, having transferred their depot in Paris to the
London Religious Tract Society, the Pearses returned to survey
Algeria. They decided to concentrate on the indigenous Berber
population called Kabyles in that part of North Africa. Accord-
ingly, they bought a half acre of land near the village of Djemaa
Sahridj and built a small house on the land. Thus, at age 65,

George Pearse became the first missionary of a Mission family which has continued over a hundred years.

On his return to England he passed through Europe and enlisted as his first missionary colleague a young Swiss named Henri Mayor. Upon arriving in England he began the study of the Kabyle language and wrote a booklet entitled, "Mission to the Kabyles" in order to inform and challenge Christians regarding the neglect of North Africa. He also met Mr. Glenny who had been recommended to him by Dr. Guinness. A fourth member of this first party was a former student of Dr. Guinness, a convert from Islam named Selim Zeytoun. So it was that November 5, 1881, this party arrived in Algiers and moved on to Djemaa Sahridj. The North Africa Mission was born.

Two years later Mr. Pearse handed the little Mission over to a Council in London who appointed Edward H. Glenny Honorary General Secretary. Pearse himself together with his wife moved to the city of Algiers where they continued their witness to Kabyles and engaged in the distribution of literature for several more years. As time went on, however, the health of both failed and they had to return to England. Finally, June 30, 1902, this ardent and generous servant of God "fell on sleep" aged 88.

The second member of this founding committee, Henry Grattan Guinness, was a well-known and influential Christian leader already deeply involved in missionary enterprises when the idea of missions to North Africa arose. Born in 1835 to a wealthy family in Dublin he spent the last fifty years of his life deeply involved in missionary work. His conversion was rather unusual. His younger brother had just returned from a lengthy trip at sea. During that voyage he had been converted by a shipmate. Upon returning home he enthusiastically shared his newfound faith with Grattan. Next morning, soundly converted, Grattan Guinness began a Christian life of dedicated witness which led eventually to a ministry of preaching, writing, and aiding in the organization of missionary societies as well as training missionary candidates. In this he was ably assisted by his wife who was herself an exceptional writer and speaker. For nearly twenty years they traveled together all over the United Kingdom, Europe, and North America. Among the works they founded was the East London Institute. By the time they became interested in North Africa they had already sent out one hundred and forty-four men into missionary service through that Institute. Many more were to follow; several to North Africa.

Dr. Guinness had visited Algeria in 1879 in connection with a trip to France to see some of his students. So when Mr. Pearse told of his visit to Algeria in 1876, Dr. Guinness urged him to give himself to beginning an evangelistic work among the Berber population there and at the same time made a gift of 100 pounds to get the work started.

It takes a mighty force to overcome the inertia of centuries. And so God raised up a mighty man to mount this assault upon the citadel of Islam in North Africa. Edward Glenny was a big man, well over six feet tall, and large of frame, with prodigious energy and determination. At one and the same time he was Honorary General Secretary of the North Africa Mission, supervised several Gospel halls in the neighborhood of Barking, London, engaged in many business enterprises and also carried out an extensive ministry of writing and preaching which took him all over England and across North Africa time and again. His physical strength was matched by an unswerving faith in the Word of God and an unflagging zeal for the salvation of Muslim North Africans based upon a vital, personal walk of fellowship with the Lord. It has been justly said that what Hudson Taylor was to China, Edward Glenny was to North Africa.

It has been said that, "Grace is not hereditary, but a godly parentage is an incalculable influence for good." This was certainly the case with Mr. Glenny. His father was an earnest Christian man who spent much time in Gospel preaching, but even more in personal evangelism. Originally a member of the Church of England, he later joined the (open) Plymouth Brethren. So young Edward was brought up in an atmosphere of Bible study and personal witness.

While at school in Bristol his personal faith was strengthened under the preaching of Mr. George Mueller so that when at age 16 he had to quit school and return home to assist his father in the business, he plunged eagerly into a ministry of Bible teaching and personal witness with boys his own age which was much blessed of the Lord. As the years passed his involvement in Christian work grew steadily. In fact, when only twenty-one years old he was invited to serve as a missionary to Burma. But, due to his father's advanced age, it seemed best for the son to stay at home and assist in carrying on the business.

One day eight years later the young man read an article in the *Daily Chronicle* describing developments in Algeria, a French colony just over fifty years old. It was suggested that agricultural schemes in Algeria might well produce exports for English markets. This appealed to Glenny's business sense, since he was already engaged in market gardening. But as he read on about the country and its people, bound by the false religion of Islam, he became even more interested in the possibility of mission work there.

Accordingly he inquired of Mrs. Grattan Guinness who, with her husband, had earlier visited Algeria, to find out more about the situation there. She, in turn, referred him to Mr. George Pearse, an old friend of his (Glenny's) father's, and this led to his joining the little party which established the first station of the Mission to the Kabyles (the original name of the North Africa Mission) in November 1881.

As the youngest of the three founders of the mission Mr. Glenny was appointed Honorable General Secretary at age 29, a post he held for the next forty-three years, with the exception of almost three years, 1902-5, when a serious breakdown in health set him aside. In 1914 he suffered a slight stroke leaving him with partial paralysis of the face. And on May 13, 1924, failing health necessitated his resignation from the Mission. He died January 7, 1926.

THE HOME BASE

When Mr. Glenny returned from Algeria he set up the operational headquarters in his home at 21 Linton Road, Barking. From here he maintained correspondence with the growing group of interested friends in England and developed plans for regular visits to homes and churches in order to widen

the base of supporters. Little by little this base expanded until
twenty years later it consisted, in addition to the Glenny home,
of five other small houses where new candidates and missionaries on furlough stayed. He also gathered a considerable staff
to help train missionary recruits. Mr. and Mrs. Dovey served as
supervisors of the homes and office in order to lighten Mr.
Glenny's load and free him for visits to the field and for
deputation. Mr. Milton Marshall, formerly a missionary in
Tlemcen, Algeria from 1887-1891 and a good linguist who had
to return to England because of his wife's health, became the
professor of French and Arabic in residence until 1911. All new
recruits in those early days spent about a year at the Barking
headquarters. They not only studied Arabic but engaged in
Christian service through the four small Chapels under Mr.
Glenny's supervision. The Mission has never since enjoyed
such a comprehensive training program lasting so long to
prepare recruits for service in North Africa.

In 1902 the Mission moved to an office building at 34
Paternoster Row while one house was retained in Barking for
storage purposes. Five years later the office moved to No. 4
Highbury Crescent, a house with more commodious quarters
and less rent. Another five years and, at the request of the
landlord, the Mission vacated the premises at Highbury Crescent and moved again to "a more central position" at 18 John
Street, Bedford Row. After nearly twenty years "the cloud
moved" again. This time a combination of circumstances
enabled the Mission to sell the house in Bedford Row and with
the proceeds erase a bank loan of 3000 pounds and occupy a new
home in Highgate at no cost. Mr. F. E. Marsh, senior member
of the Council, had purchased the home at 34 Bisham Gardens,
Highgate, and donated it as a memorial to his late wife. And so
here the office of the Mission remained until it was moved north
to Loughborough.

For many years the London office directed the affairs of the
Mission and Mr. Glenny not only assumed responsibility for
the ministry of deputation throughout Britain but also made
frequent visits to the field. It is no small tribute to the skill and
dedication of this unique servant of God that the work grew so
rapidly. But by 1904 Mr. Glenny's health was weakened so by

this hard pace that he was forced to give up much of his daily
responsibilities to the supervision of Rev. William Fuller-Gooch
who then assumed the role of Honorary Secretary. A short time
later Mr. Milton Marshall shared these duties as Acting
Secretary. In 1916 Mr. Harvey Farmer took over as Assistant
Secretary to Mr. Glenny and eight years later succeeded him as
Honorary Secretary. Three years later Mr. Farmer made his
first trip to North America. He returned in 1930 and spent most
of the rest of his life as Honorary Secretary to the American
Auxiliary. In 1921 the major leadership of NAM at home and
abroad was discharged by Rev. E. J. Poole-Coonor, an unusually gifted preacher, widely known throughout Britain. But in
1930 he resigned to assume a pastorate, though remaining on
the Council. In 1939 Rev. Thomas Warren, a missionary from
Algeria who first went out to North Africa in 1911, was
appointed Field Superintendent. It appears that Field Councils
were instituted at the same time. The Field Councils, elected by
the missionaries in their regions, gave oversight to the place-
ment of personnel and opening of stations. The Field Superintendent, in turn, provided liason between the Field Councils
and the individual missionaries, on the one hand, and the Home
Council on the other. This was a big step forward. It met a
growing need for closer supervision and direction of the work
based on better intelligence gathered by a competent field man
who was thoroughly acquainted with the problems by personal
experience. It also went a long way toward answering criticisms
of interdenominational missions that the NAM lacked the
cohesion and coordination that a denominational mission provides. At the same time Mr. Warren received his new appointment, the Council also appointed Mr. Oswald L. Carnegie, a
business man and member of the Council, as Honorary Secretary; the first permanent appointment since the death of Mr.
Glenny in 1926.

In 1945, while Mr. Carnegie continued on for a while as
Honorary Secretary, Mr. Ernest J. Long was appointed General Secretary to take more immediate direction of affairs in the
London office. He had already served for many years in Tunisia
and Algeria and since his return home had been for some time
editing the News Letter. Now he assumed further duties

regarding deputation and other business matters. He continued in this job, with the exception of a few years during the War, until retirement in 1965. At that time Rev. Robert Brown took over and carried on in the London office until he resigned to assume the pastorate of Highgate Road Baptist Church in 1972. He was succeeded by Rev. Ronald Waine. Mr. Waine had earlier served in the Algiers Mission Band so he was well acquainted with mission work among North Africans. At the time of his appointment he was on the staff of All Nations Bible College teaching mission courses.

EARLY GROWTH

The beginning in 1881 was a shaky one. Within a year both Zeytoun and Mayor had resigned and left the country. There was constant surveillance and interference from the French authorities which made their work very difficult. However Henri Mayor returned a little later on as an independent, located in a Kabyle village and carried on for nearly fifty years.

The vacancy left by these men was filled immediately, if temporarily, by two English ladies and a year later by Mr. and Mrs. Lamb. Soon thereafter another Swiss missionary, M. Eugene Cuendet joined the team at Djemaa Sahridj. From that time on until after Algerian independence this station in Kabylia was continuously occupied. In 1883 there was a reorganization of the "Mission to the Kabyles." The name was changed to "Mission to the Kabyles and Other Races," and a larger Council was formed. By 1888 the name became the North Africa Mission.

There was astonishingly rapid growth from 1883 onwards. Algiers was occupied that year and Tlemcen the following year. Constantine and Oran were added in 1886 and Cherchell in 1890. So in nine years most of the major centers in Algeria were centers of missionary work. Djemaa Sahridj was always and only a focus for Berber witness. In later years Mekla (1920) and Azazga (1925) in Greater Kabylia were added. And at the beginning the focus in Algiers itself was Kabyle work although this was later broadened to include speakers of Arabic.

Tangier was entered in 1884 by the famous E. J. Baldwin (of

whom more later) and by 1900 Fes, Tetuan and Casablanca were added. In Tunisia NAM missionaries entered Tunis in 1885 very shortly after it had been "liberated" from economic chaos by French soldiers. And by 1900 Sfax, Sousse, Kairouan and Bizerte were also occupied as was Tripoli in Libya (1889) and three places in Egypt (Alexandria 1892, Rosetta 1897, and Sehbin el-Kom 1899). A short-lived effort, avowedly to reach bedouin, began in 1886 in what was then known as Syria. But it never really amounted to much and ceased entirely by 1892.

However, after only nineteen years the North Africa Mission had grown from nothing to 115 missionaries in 17 centers in the countries of Morocco, Algeria, Tunisia, Libya and Egypt. Surely this is evidence of the Holy Spirit's blessing upon the vision of Pearse and Guinness and especially the leadership of Edward Glenny. In order fully to appreciate the significance of this first steady growth it is important to remember that previously relatively little consideration was given to North Africa as a mission field by anybody and even less interest was shown in the evangelizing of Muslims there.

Shortly after 1900 there was a general decline in the fortunes of the Mission till it bottomed out at around 63 people in 1913. Then there was another climb after World War I to a peak of nearly 100 around 1930. Then another slump, accelerated by World War II and the post-war problems in Britain, brought the number of personnel down to just over 60 by 1947.

In 1952 the first Field Administration was established with Rev. Harold Stalley as Field Director. He was soon joined by Rev. Robert Brown as Deputy Field Director. As the International Council assigned increasing authority to the Field leader the name of the office changed from Field Director to Secretary General to International Secretary until finally it became General Director with the appointment of Rev. Abram Wiebe in 1977. Field Headquarters had already been located in Aix-en-Provence, France one year earlier.

It is difficult to portray the growth of the work in a simple manner for the plain reason that the numbers fluctuate so much. In terms of personnel this fluctuation results largely from the fact that sickness was so much more prevalent in early days, and especially mortal sickness, so that even with a

relatively constant addition of recruits the total varied. Added
to deaths, resignations also caused a considerable drop. The
general trend, however, may be followed and matched with
major political and economic factors in Europe.

But when it comes to reporting the number of occupied
stations, there are additional problems. What actually consti-
tutes an occupied station? Does a visit for several weeks or a
few months? Internal political and military exigencies in North
Africa often caused missionaries to abandon their homes for
short periods of time.

Ideally six to eight people consitute the basic number of
personnel for an adequately staffed station; two married
couples and two to four single workers. This number will ensure
continued operation of the station when some of the staff are on
furlough. It also permits team work in which the several
members can share their individual talents cooperatively. Furthermore, the group can strengthen one another against the
satanic pressures of work in a Muslim land and by their
presence they already consitute the local church which should
be the foundation for the later independent national church.

In October of 1900 Mr. Glenny wrote a general survey of the
progress of the work of the Mission at that point. Since they
were entering a new century he apparently felt that such a
review was appropriate. Speaking of support he noted that
more than twelve hundred donations had been made; the
largest was a legacy of 1729 pounds from a kind friend "who
had only given a few shillings during his lifetime, so that his
bequest was quite unexpected." Nearly one thousand gifts were
of five pounds or under. Gifts came from people in eighteen
countries and, as an example of true brotherhood, from the
missionaries of five different Societies. All this illustrated the
broad base of support established after less than twenty years.

But of greater importance he addressed himself to the
perplexing problem of limited visible results. His thoughts are
so cogent and so eloquently expressed, they should be quoted
verbatim.

We rejoice that we have a few converts from Islam who give us encouragement, and are seeking to spread the Gospel, and others who profess conversion, some of whom seem to be making progress, though some, alas! deceive us or go back. When we take into consideration the difficulties of the sphere, and the way in which God seems generally to work in these days, we think substantial progress is being made.

God could, if He saw fit, enable missionaries to know Arabic without study, and empower them to heal the sick without years spent in studying medicine. He seems, however, rather to encourage the use of ordinary means, but grants the help of His gracious Spirit to assist our natural powers. This may be a slower process than the former, but does it not call for a greater exercise of the graces of patience and perseverance, which are of higher value than mere power? A very eminent and holy servant of Christ has pointed out that God often answers the prayers of young believers more quickly than those of older ones, because He knows their weaknesses and inability to wait, and does not desire to discourage them. May not His dealings with the Church as a whole be similar? May not the rapid successes of the early Church have been granted to encourage young and weak communities, while the slower progress we sometimes complain of is permitted, because, with all the glorious experiences of God's faithfulness to past generations, we are expected to have grace to wait more patiently than they for blessing not less sure?

Let us have patience as well as faith. On the last occasion on which I heard the aged and venerable George Mueller, he exhorted us by prayer and faith and *patience* to seek from God whatever we might need. So also during an interview with the veteran African missionary, Robert Moffat, a few months before he died, he said to me,

"I think the work you have in North Africa is
harder than what I had in South Africa, if I
may judge from the Moslems I have met, and
you will need patience, patience, patience;"
and this is the testimony of every foreign missionary
of experience. Only let us beware lest under the plea
of patience we disguise indifference or unbelief.

May we heed these wise words of advice from the founder of
our Mission as we enter the second century of our history.

IMAGINATIVE STRATEGIES

Two quite unusual programs for missionary work arose in
those early years; one eccentric, the other exemplary. The
eccentric plan was derived by Mr. Baldwin from his interpretation of principles in the tenth chapter of Matthew. The exemplary plan was a scheme of supervised literature distribution
and Bible teaching far in advance of its time. Miss Emma
Herdman gets credit for this one. But first, Mr. Baldwin and
Matthew X.
It all began in Tangier. Mr. E. F. Baldwin, a Southern
Baptist preacher from North Carolina, was the first NAM
missionary in Morocco. While Mr. Baldwin was holding meetings in Virginia in the Fall of 1883 he read in *The Christian*, a
London weekly magazine, about the Kabyles of North Africa.
He went to Richmond and presented this information as a
project to the Southern Baptist Board of Foreign Missions. The
Board, impressed by Baldwin's report, sent him for a visit to
Kabylia. Upon his return to the States, Baldwin presented a
long, detailed report (including notices of baptisms he had
performed) to the convention meeting in Baltimore. However,
his plan was rejected. The Convention decided instead to
extend their work in Mexico. But Mr. Baldwin was not about to
be put off. He had met members of the NAM in Algeria, so he
applied and went out to North Africa under that Mission. In
1884 the Baldwin family, eleven in all, arrived in Tangier. He
was persuaded by Mr. Glenny to remain in Morocco. Mrs.

Baldwin's father was a doctor so she had picked up some medical knowledge at home. On this basis she began a limited medical ministry in Tangier which later became the Tulloch Memorial Hospital. After three years the Baldwins resigned from NAM to begin free lance work in Fes further south. While there arrangements were made for him to assist the first recruits of the newly formed Southern Morocco Mission. Mr. Baldwin was a most enthusiastic and optimistic man. He reported results everywhere he went. It was said of him, not altogether facetiously, that he preached to men on Friday, baptized them on Saturday, admitted them to the Lord's table on Sunday and then sent them out as missionaries!

All of a sudden Mr. Baldwin dropped his bomb. He wrote a series of articles for *The Christian* in which he enunciated what he claimed were the true biblical principles for missionary work. These, he said, he had found in the words of instruction which Jesus gave His disciples as recorded in the tenth chapter of Matthew. Baldwin summarized these under five heads; 1) no certain income, 2) no possessions, 3) no provision for bodily care, 4) no convenient appointment for travel and 5) separation from normal friendships. This announcement stirred quite a controversy in Christian circles and produced replies in several different Christian periodicals. One telling reply by Mrs. Grattan Guinness pointed out that Jesus also limited the scope of witness at that time to Israel only by adding, "Go not into the way of the Gentiles." It is enough to point out the insufficiency of such principles in that they required constant travel, always dependent upon native strangers for hospitality, and allowed no proper opportunity for systematic teaching or training of inquirers or converts. Baldwin's amazing results, as he reported them, seemed to give some validity to his claims. But, as local pressure against him mounted and his unpopularity grew, he left for Syria.

In the final analysis, although his theory was wrong, his enthusiasm was unbounded and infectious. Since he helped some of the new recruits of SMM in language and took them along on his evangelistic trips, he was able to get them to support his theory for a while. But eventually Mr. Anderson, the founder of SMM, fully recognizing the error of Baldwin's policy, prohibited its employment by any SMM missionaries. Nevertheless, in spite of his eccentricities, Mr. Baldwin did play a major role in getting the SMM established.

At about the same time a talented lady from England developed a remarkably imaginative plan for evangelism in Morocco. In some respects Miss Emma Herdman was one of the most unusual and gifted of the missionaries of NAM in its entire history. In fact the work she initiated and directed from Fes for just eleven years was perhaps the most successful attempt to involve national converts in evangelism anywhere in the Muslim world. It took genius, imagination, leadership, energy and faith. Miss Herdman was outstandingly gifted in all these areas.

She came from a wealthy home near Belfast, North Ireland and enjoyed fully the benefit of an extensive education to match her native talent. For several years she travelled and studied in Europe and could converse fluently in six languages in addition to her knowledge of Latin, Greek and Hebrew. But she was not just a student. She was a teacher and a skilled communicator.

Most important of all, having been brought up in a devout Christian home she received excellent training in the Bible which she put to good use following her conversion at age twenty-four. At first she served in several churches in Britain but later became associated with the Bible Society in France. Having made arrangements to work with them in Algiers she sailed for Gibraltar in 1884. However, since an epidemic of cholera had temporarily halted sea traffic to Algiers, Miss Herdman, never one to remain idle, went across to Tangier. Here she met the people of NAM and was drawn by compassion for the Moroccans she saw to get involved in a ministry right there. She resigned from the Bible Society and became an associate of NAM.

After a period of studying Arabic and gaining experience in working with Muslims in the Tangier area she set out with a companion, Miss Caley, to a new work in the town of Arsila thirty miles south of Tangier. Next year they moved further south to Larash. Again, the following year, Miss Herdman in a party of four women visited Fes, the northern capital of Morocco and the main center of Muslim education. Apparently, the strategic situation of Fes appealed to her as a good place from which to reach out for evangelism. It seems evident that as she viewed the situation and considered plans which would enhance the spread of the Gospel she thought of multiplying her efforts by training associates. Being a skilled teacher and realizing that in a Muslim society men were best fitted to reach the upper classes and command their attention to the message, she set out to find and train Christian men as colporteurs and teachers.

Thus began this unique ministry. Assisted by a nurse, Miss Copping, for a simple medical service and another associate Miss Reed, Emma Herdman gathered together a team of Moroccan men to travel widely through northern Morocco selling Christian literature and teaching Bible. It is quite plain that Miss Herdman was the leader. She was old enough to command the respect of Moroccan men and gain their confidence in her authority. She made sure as best she could that the men were genuine Christians. She gave sound Bible instruction. And she directed their travels carefully and thoughtfully.

Nevertheless, some people were skeptical about the reliability of this scheme and the validity of its results. Therefore she was reluctant to publish statistics and careful to keep close contact with the workers. There are reports of this work in successive issues of the NAM magazine but it is evident that the purpose of these reports was more to encourage prayer than to cite success. It is important to keep in mind two aspects of this ministry especially as it took place before 1900. First, sound doctrinal teaching accompanied the distribution of literature. Second, a lady missionary not only ministered to Moroccan men, she directed their activities.

Saturday 15 April 1899, Miss Herdman became violently ill. When it was decided to take her to Tangier the party set out with the patient in a mule litter for a long trip. However, the strain on her was too great, and so early in the morning six days later she died while the party was still about forty miles short of their destination. Two other missionaries stepped in to carry on this work of which there was still notice in the magazine as late as 1909. Then it apparently came to an end.

This unique program was a distinct advance on previous

methods of evangelism among Muslims. It contained advanced training in "theology" as opposed to simple "Gospel"; it multiplied its effectiveness by involving many national associates and it included trained nationals directly in the ministry of the Word. If only there had been a program to gather the fruit of this ministry into worshipping groups which could have been prepared for responsible leadership! But it is unfair to criticise the program for neglecting what no other was doing at that time either. Instead, we admire the vision and ability of a missionary who was thinking well ahead of her time.

IMPRESSIONS OF THE FIELD

What is it like trying to reach Muslim people living not only in large crowded cities but also in the smaller towns and villages in North Africa? How does one get started; what can you do? Permit me to let Pastor James Stephens tell you in his report of a visit to North Africa in 1890. Things have changed a good deal since then especially in the technical fields; it takes only a few hours today to make a trip that required a week or more before. Social conditions also are much improved. But the main problems remain. And in any case his report accurately summarizes the situation for at least the first half of our history.

Pastor Stephens, long a close friend and Council member of NAM, was a leading figure in evangelical circles in England. He pastored Highgate Road Baptist Church in London. His teaching and personal influence not only turned many persons to missionary service but also people interested in missions came from all over England to the church for training which would confirm to them God's call to the field. Mr. Stephens was not a theoretician. He knew what he was talking about. And his report gives clear, concise insight into the problems of his day.

In an article entitled, "Some Impressions of a Visit to Algeria" he writes:

> I had the privilege, in company with Mr. Glenny
> and Mrs. Bridgford, of seeing and conferring with all
> the North Africa Mission workers in Algeria. I was

not able to accompany my friends east to Tunis and
Tripoli, or west to Morocco; so anything I have to
say has reference exclusively to Algeria.

The French rule in Algeria has brought about the
settlement there of many French people, as well as
Spaniards. These are found not only in the cities and
towns, but in small distinctly French villages, over
the whole of the country. Much of the land that is
best for cultivation is in the hands of French cultiva-
tors. Algiers and other leading places are in great
part European cities. Well-made European roads are
found over the extent of the colony; and between
1000 and 2000 miles of railway have been constructed. Of course, in a French village of any size a French
hotel can be found. In this way the conditions of life
and travel for missionaries are much more European
than one generally associates with the name of
Africa.

The greater part of the native population is Arab,
so-called. But there is a considerable proportion
which is Kabyle or Berber. The latter are regarded as
the aboriginal inhabitants, and are found principally
in mountainous parts. Their language is quite distinct from the Arabs. The Kabyle men often leave
their homes in the mountains, temporarily, in search
of work in the cities and towns. A stranger at first
can hardly distinguish between Arab and Berber,
when he sees them in the crowded thoroughfares.

In the towns there is a very mixed population. The
native houses are principally found in one quarter.
They are altogether oriental in form and arrangement.

The natives who live in the country have not such
houses as the natives in the towns. As one travels
along the line through long stretches of country that
seem uninhabited, he has pointed out to him, here
and there, clusters of poor looking hovels, the walls
of which may be five feet high, or may at times be
only three. Or, again, he sees a cluster of dark tents,

like a gypsy encampment. These are the native villages. Hundreds of thousands live in these; yet withal the country is very sparsely inhabited.

The work of our missionary brethren and sisters is in the towns, except in the case of those who work in the mountains of Kabylia. The missionaries are all able to speak French, which, of course, is the language of business and travel; but as their aim is to reach the native population, they have had to acquire Arabic or Kabyle as well.

It is hardly possible for the missionaries to live in the little native villages. These must be reached by visits. As the distances are great, and the heat fatiguing, it is almost indispensable that the missionary should have a horse or mule. Without such an aid his work would be, in comparison, most limited.

There is not in Algeria the facility for open-air work that there is in many mission fields. Of course, in a small cluster of purely native dwellings one might be permitted to speak to the men openly. But wherever one is under the observation of the French authorities the open-air preaching would be disallowed.

Again, there is not the scope for Tract and Bible distribution that is sometimes found in other fields. It is not that one is forbidden to distribute, but that so few of the natives can read. In one district it was told me that probably only one in fifty could read.

How, then, can the workers get openings for their work?

The missionary *brethren* are precluded from visiting the homes of the people, neither could they get meetings among them; therefore they are obliged to seek to fulfil their commission by speaking to men individually by the way, or by going into public cafes, and there getting into talk with the leisurely frequenters.

The *sisters* have found access to houses to visit the

women. Having once had an invitation to a house, their friendliness, the interest attaching to them, and their ability to suggest simple medical help, not only open the way for repeated return to the house, but open the way to other houses. And thus they have secured openings for the Gospel.

There has been some advance in work among the young. By dint of much persevering, loving effort, classes of girls have been got, and, along with the sewing taught, hymns and texts have been impressed on the memory. In like manner classes of boys have been gathered. Subsidiary to the work among the natives, the missionaries take advantage of opportunities among the French and Spanish.

There has been, on the whole a hopeful beginning of work made, but as yet only a beginning. As one looks with his own eyes on the circumstances, he does not wonder that there has not been more progress, but rather is thankful for what there has been. At the same time his heart is stirred as he thinks of cities with tens of thousands of inhabitants, and perhaps not more than six or eight or a dozen regenerate people in each—stirred to earnest prayer, and to zeal as regards further possible methods of service.

There has been some fruit, and at the same time very real impression made. But there is occasion for much persistent keeping at it in godly hopefulness, in spite of almost universal indifference and opposedness. The common observation was, "There is so little conviction of sin." Even when some few have said that they believed in Jesus, and have shown some evidence of it in their lives, there has not been a break with Mohammedanism: there has not been getting baptized, nor breaking from the observance of the fast of Ramadan. Two or three exceptions to this have gladdened the hearts of the missionaries. The difficulty, however, of open confession seems to be a very real one, and connects itself with the thought of positive danger to life.

Under these circumstances I felt how greatly it
behooved the Christians to sympathize with our
workers. It is far harder to work on as they do than
when there is the joy of many conversions and open
confessions. They are there because our Lord wants
them there. Their earnestness, and their spirituality,
and their purposefulness, gladden the visitor's heart.
We cannot doubt that they shall reap if they faint
not.

The years to come will be freed from some difficulties that the years of their starting on work brought
with them. And, besides, they will have increased in
acquaintance with God.

I felt convinced of the benefit of a visit to the field.
The missionaries themselves appreciated and got
cheer from the presence and converse of Christians
from home. And the Christians from home could
understand with clearness and vividness the difficulties of the work, the value of what had been done,
and the claims of the workers on loving encouragement and wise sympathy. If some friends could pay
such a visit, their own missionary interest would be
very definitely deepened. Indeed, I do not doubt that
if some could see for themselves the field, they would
desire to settle in it for work.

PROBLEMS WITH GOVERNMENTS

From the very beginning the NAM missionaries faced problems with the governing officials in the countries where they
worked. These problems, however, were different from those
faced by missionaries in sub-Saharan Africa. There it was, at
the first at least, the petty African kings and local tribal chiefs
who strongly resisted the intrusion of foreigners. However, by
the time European countries had wrested control from native
rulers and replaced them with colonial officers political problems for missionaries were reduced or eliminated; especially for
British missionaries in British colonies. North of the Sahara

British missionaries contended with a long independent Muslim Sultanate in Morocco, Turkish Pashas in Tripoli and hostile French authorities in Algeria and Tunisia. Morocco presented problems chiefly because the central government rarely exercised effective control over the country beyond the major cities. So local Berber chiefs sometimes included the foreigners in their harassment of all outside control. However, in the early days although the Sultan's governors often delayed or discouraged missionaries from travelling too far into the countryside, for the most part the travellers were cordially received by the people when they went; partly out of curiosity but also because of the medical ministry they sometimes performed—albeit largely the distribution of simple remedies for the multitudes of ailing people and antiseptic dressings for every kind of infection or wound. The Moroccan people were deeply impressed by the evident concern for their needs and interest in them personally which the missionaries so genuinely demonstrated.

In 1907 there was outbreak of violence which seems to have resulted largely as a reaction of the tribespeople to the interference of French troops or from resentment that the Sultan used these foreign troops to extend control over Moroccan tribal soldiers. The situation appears to have developed from the deliberate policy of the Sultan to exploit the jealousies of European powers concerning their influence in Morocco by playing one off against the other and using the one most amenable to him as an aid in subduing rebellious tribes. The result was that the general population, including missionaries, found themselves caught in between the two forces. On this particular occasion French sailors, invited by the Sultan's officials, had landed to put down local disorder in Casablanca and were fired on by tribal soldiers. Accordingly, French warships in the harbor bombarded the town. Finally, the tribesmen ran wild looting and burning through the city. Through it all innocent citizens both Moroccan and European suffered (many were kidnapped and carried away to the hills) and the small NAM hospital was demolished; but the missionaries were all spared. A few months later when tension relaxed the missionaries were back on the job again.

On another occasion a few years later missionaries in the city of Fes were isolated by rebelling tribesmen supporting an usurper from the south. For a while, it was feared that no roads of escape were safe but eventually all got away and when things quieted down they, too, returned to their posts.

Little by little, France, bargaining with Spain and Germany for influence in other parts of Africa, gained the right to move into Morocco alone, so by 1912 they established a protectorate "assisting" the Moroccan monarch in the governing of his realm and setting about to maintain order and develop the natural resources of the country. However, it was a long drawn out program which really only ended when all armed resistance ceased in 1934.

Missionary activity was relatively unhindered at the beginning in Tunisia. The Turkish governors (Beys) in Tunis were not faced with anything like the resistance of the Berber tribes in Morocco. So when French troops moved into Tunisia in 1881 in order to stabilize its economy, an arrangement was quickly reached which led to improved economic policy and continued development of societal structures.

Morever, since medical facilities were still sparse, missionaries found many opportunities to use medicine in one form or another as a means to win acceptance. There was less reluctance to grant permission, for Tunisia was not a part of France as Algeria was. Therefore governmental interference was no great problem in the early years. When Tunisia gained independence, however, the strengthening of native cultural elements throughout the country, such as the Arabic language, also included expanding Islam as the national religion. This has, of course, resulted in curtailing many missionary functions such as the operation of book stores, wide scale sale of literature, etc. which were popular before.

But from the very beginning there were more conflicts with government in Algeria than anywhere else. In the first place, France had annexed Algeria nearly fifty years before the first missionaries arrived. Both NAM and Algiers Mission Band, among the first to arrive, were essentially British and Protestant. This naturally led Roman Catholic France from suspicion to action. Three times, in 1896 and again in 1901 and 1904, deputies from some of the Departments in Algeria made charges in the Chamber of Deputies in Paris against the missionaries in Algeria. These charges ranged from espionage as such to distributing arms and gunpowder to nationals. At first, because of anti-British feelings generally in France, the attacks received a favorable response and repressive measures were taken to curtail the activities of the missionaries. And since the charges were made by representatives of the Departments of Constantine and Oran in Algeria these regions felt the blow most strongly. Several of the missionaries had to leave their stations and properties were abandoned temporarily. But soon reason returned and relative quiet was restored. After a while when the baselessness of the charges became apparent a reaction set in. This was supported by a letter the Synod of the French Reformed Church sent to Paris in 1904. The French pastors in Algeria knew the British missionaries and commended them for unselfish service to the government. Relations between the French authorities and British subjects improved even more after the Entente Cordiale of April 8th that same year.

In Algeria, as elsewhere in North Africa, it was only after the newly independent government began to extend its control throughout the country that increasing pressure upon missionary activity developed again.

THE GREAT WAR

The Great War, as World War I was known at the time, did not have a very serious effect on mission work in North Africa. For one thing the European powers in control of North Africa, France and Italy, were among the Allies rather than, as in the case of World War II, when both Vichy France and especially Italy were ranged with Germany against Great Britain. In fact, the missionaries had reported a decided change for the better in the attitude of French authorities in North Africa ever since the 1904 Entente Cordiale which united Britain and France in the face of their common foe Germany. Travel by sea was, of course, somewhat hazardous since German submarines roamed the shipping lanes and many Allied ships were sunk. But this was no more than an inconvenience to missionaries travelling by sea from England to Morocco or across the Mediterranean from France either to Algeria or Tunisia. Some mention is made in the Mission magazine of the hardships of rationing but finances seemed to flow in as regularly as before the war. New recruits were occasionally sent out to the field and the work continued nearly as normal.

To be sure some essential commodities were either hard to get or unavailable. In addition, the black market prices kept soaring and the purchasing power of the pound diminished since it was pegged to a weakening franc. At the Christmas season in 1919 it was devalued from 200 to 480 per pound providing welcome relief for the missionaries. Now it only cost 25 shillings to have a pair of shoes repaired in Tunis instead of three pounds.

There is one interesting bit of information, however, in the October-November issue of *North Africa*. In the middle of one column of Mr. Glenny's report "To the Friends of the North Africa Mission" there appears what seemed to me at first to be a picture of a geometrical design, perhaps a rug pattern. Upon closer examination it proved to be a solid print-over to block out thirteen lines of type. My curiosity aroused, I studied this section carefully with a magnifying glass and deciphered the message which a military censor had thought it unwise to publish but which any enterprising reader, or German spy, could have found out by employing the same method I did. Mr. Glenny had simply reported the narrow escape of his house from a (fire) bomb as follows:

> On the 17th August the Zeppelin bomb fell within twenty feet of this house and got our neighbor's fence on fire but this was soon put out. It was a merciful escape . . . as had it fallen about a second sooner it would probably have gone through the roof of our house and set it on fire. As it was, it was very trying to the nerves especially of the ladies of the house. This is the third Zeppelin raid I have been in here or elsewhere but not one single shaft can hit until the God of love sees fit.

Censored, perhaps, because the authorities did not want Germany to find out what effect on morale the Zeppelin raids had made.

Thousands of North Africans served in the French forces. Among them were the "goums" of Morocco and Algeria (or levees; both words mean, literally, "get up"). Many were Christians. In fact, several known personally to the missionaries laid down their lives in battle. Two of the NAM missionaries served with the forces. Dr. James Liley served as an Army Scripture Reader with the British troops. And Mr. Cyril Morriss also a Scripture Reader died while in service in Beirut, Lebanon.

3

PRESSING ON: 1932—1945

"PATIENCE OF HOPE"

Remembering without ceasing your *work of faith* and your *labor of love* and your *patience of hope.*" Those are the three needful ingredients that we should always maintain in our service for God.

One of the things that struck me as I went into the harder fields amongst the Moslems was how many of these missionaries, by the grace of God, carry on there with the *patience of hope.* They are always expecting to see a break and to reap a harvest, and I am quite certain that is true in the North Africa Mission.

Dr. Northcote Deck,
North Africa, December 1931

A PRAYER FOR MOSLEMS

O God, Who once didst make Thy ways
By Israel's prophets known,
And unto us in later days
Hast spoken in Thy Son,
We pray Thee multitudes to turn
From Islam's shadows dim
To hail Thy Prophet's light, and learn
The way of truth from Him.

O God, Whose Son presents His prayers
In priestly raiment dressed,
Who pleads His once shed blood, and bears
Our names upon His breast,
Look Thou on those whose hopeless creed
His blessed Cross denies,
Unseal their eyes to see their need
Of Priest and Sacrifice.

For He shall come, Thy Son by Whom
The ages Thou hast made,
Whose advent-trumpet sounds the doom
Of all 'gainst Thee arrayed;
O God, ere Thy dread judgments fall
Do Thou in mercy bring
A ransomed host from Islam's thrall
To serve the Saviour King.

E. J. Poole-Connor

THE JUBILEE

In 1931 the NAM celebrated its golden jubilee. Fifty years of missionary endeavor in North Africa came to an end.* This might be a good time to take stock of developments not only in NAM but in the world at large as they relate to missions.

The period of world-wide rapid economic growth following the Great War had suffered its first devastating blow through the 1929 crash in America. And shock waves were spreading

---

* *Incidentally, three years later the senior missionary on the field, Mr. Eugene Cuendet, a Swiss, celebrated his jubilee of service.*

around the world. Soon Nazism in Germany and Fascism in Italy would grow like morbid cancers. In a few years the first rumblings of world-wide conflict would be heard: Japan in China in 1937 and Germany in Austria in 1938.

At the same time even more ominous events were taking place. There was a steady creeping erosion in the theological vitality of missions. Evangelical convictions were under attack. Ever since the Edinburgh Conference of 1910 a process of theological dilution continued to undermine the foundations of evangelical missions. The second World Council, held at Jerusalem in 1928, marked further departure from the biblical basis of an authoritative Scripture. The impact of theological liberalism favored an emphasis on social concerns at the expense of personal salvation.

These world trends seem to have had little effect directly upon the work in North Africa. It took time for the theological poison of liberalism to trickle down to the field; and even when it did reach North Africa it affected only some of the denominational leaders and their programs. But there is little doubt that the major effect was to dampen evangelistic concern and inhibit participation in missions on the part of the home churches. Not only was the personal spiritual commitment of Christians under attack but their giving in support of missions had also been considerably reduced.

It seems that God led the British leaders of NAM to anticipate these problems by sending Mr. Harvey Farmer to America in 1927 in order to enlist support for the Mission in North Africa. At any rate this marks the beginning of the partnership which has grown with the passing years.

For the most part the work on the field continued as before. The first recruits from America arrived in 1934. Several new posts were opened and two were reopened which had been unoccupied for years due to lack of workers. Hope House in Tangier received major renovations and additions including a third floor. It was set aside as both a rest home for missionaries and a guest house for Christian friends when they made visits to the field.

In this chapter we will examine more at length some of the special ministries of the Mission and also the problems attend-

ing the support of the work. But first let us take note of the
gradually changing scene on the field as it relates to the
conduct of missionary evangelism. As the North African countries were exposed more and more to outside influences there
was first of all, an increasingly open curiosity about foreign
ideas, then a gradual tightening against the threat of too many
disruptive concepts. Alert missionaries adapted to the new
climate.

HELEN MORRISS STORY

These changes can best be illustrated from the recollections
of a person whose experience on the field spans sufficient time
to have noticed them. Among many retired missionaries Mrs.
Helen Morriss (nee Helen Short) is especially well qualified to
help in this regard. Born on the field to missionary parents, she
spent her first ten years in Kairouan, Tunisia. Then after a
period in England for education she returned in 1927 as a young
woman and after marriage spent approximately ten years in
and around Nabuel, Tunisia. Home in England from 1939 until
1957 she again returned to Tunisia, this time working principally with school and college girls in Tunis until retirement in
1971. Thus her experience spans the early period of witness in
Tunisia when she was a child (1905-1915), the years between the
world wars (1927-1939) and the period of adjustment to new-
found independence (1957-1971). I believe her observations
provide us, from the perspective of one person in one country,
the pattern of development in North Africa generally. They also
help us to appreciate how the methods employed in witness by
the missionaries were modified to suit the changing social
climate as well as the developing mission program as it was
more clearly orientated toward the planting of an independent
national church.

Let us hear the story in her own words. She begins with her
parents in London.

Mr. Evan Short and Miss Beatrice Tiptaft both
joined the Mission in the days when Mr. Glenny was
father and leader of the Mission and both were in his

home. It was then virtually the candidate school. They were studying Arabic under Mr. Marshall and at the same time helping in the Christian work that Mr. Glenny was engaged in so that he was able to assess their character and abilities before he sent them out to the field to learn the language. My father was only there a few months before he went on to the field in February of 1899. My mother just met him there for a few months. She still had eight months to go before she went out in October via Marseilles to Egypt where there was a flourishing work at the time.

My father began to want a wife, and looking down the list of available young ladies on the list of the North Africa Mission, Miss Beatrice Tiptaft came into his mind as a very suitable young lady. He wrote to her asking if she would consider corresponding with him. Well, of course, she wrote back very properly and said she really didn't know him but would like to know him a little more before even corresponding with him. So he promptly wrote up to Mr. Glenny in great secrecy to ask if he could be transferred to Egypt. Well, Mr. Glenny didn't keep the secret very well, but anyhow my father was moved to Egypt and greatly profited by the opportunities for continued language study there. My mother was in Alexandria but, of course, my father was not posted there. They were not allowed to even be in the same town. He was in Shebin el Kom. He had a good period of Arabic study and at the same time was able to court my mother. So they were able to get to know one another. Their love deepened and they were married 10th of October, 1901 in Alexandria and then were transferred back to Constantine where my father had previously been working for about a year. Their next appointment was to the city of Kairouan in Tunisia where there was no male missionary.

My earliest connection with the North Africa

Mission began in 1905 when I was born in the holy
city of Kairouan. My earliest recollections were not
very glamourous. Insect life abounded. There were
fleas and flies and many other varieties of insects.
The town was very hot in the summer months of the
year. I can remember even today my revulsion as a
little child at all the dirt in the streets, the physical
deformities of the people, the repulsive beggars that
abounded. Food was not very plentiful and rather
limited in scope and we often had periods of financial
shortage. But through all this my parents kept on in
that town through the grace of God for twenty years.

The environment around was very hostile with
considerable religious opposition. In my early years I
can remember boys in the street calling out to my
parents and throwing stones at them.

We lived in a big old Arab house right in the heart
of the native quarter. I can remember, especially in
the hot weather, so many children coming with sore
eyes and my mother putting drops in their eyes. In
that way, by patience and love they won the trust
and affection of many of the people there.

For girls, there were classes four mornings a week
in which they learned embroidery and sewing; and
then had a good solid time of teaching. Of course,
they were quite illiterate. Everything had to be
taught to them by memory; Scripture verses, Christian hymns and Bible stories.

One day a week there was a class for women and
one morning each week—on Friday mornings—a
class for boys. These were usually a rather rough lot
but my father persevered with them.

For men, my father had a little book shop where he
would receive them, although not many were literate.
But there were Scriptures and tracts and booklets for
those who could read and it was also a good place for
discussion. In the evening, he would hold lantern
meetings showing the old glass slides in what we
used to call the magic lantern. He would usually

begin with a parable or an Old Testament story. But
as soon as he would start to speak of Jesus Christ or
the death of Christ all of his audience would walk
out. These were the days, of course, before the
movies so the picture stories were very attractive
and interesting.

But as far as converts standing; we did not see a
single one.

It was a lonely life. Tunis was a good many
train-ride hours away and Mother very rarely went
up there. She couldn't leave us children and transport in general was very difficult in the early days.
So they enjoyed very little Christian fellowship. It
was wonderful the way the Lord sustained their faith
and courage and enabled them to hold on.

My next period with the North Africa Mission was
when I joined the Mission and went out to the field in
1927. In late 1929 I was married to Mr. Cyril Morriss
who had joined the Mission four years earlier. We
were married in the city of Tunis and shortly after
went to settle in the little coastal town of Nabeul.

Missionary work was still very, very difficult. The
French gave us freedom to work. But the women and
girls were completely under the domination of the
menfolk. However, Nabeul had already been opened
up a bit by previous missionaries so it didn't take me
long to start classes for little girls and shortly after
that a women's class. But this was still in the days
when women were completely shut in. You might get
a little girl coming along at the age of about ten and
just when her mind was beginning to be really
receptive she would come along one day and say,
"My father says I mustn't go out any more." From
that time on she was shut in just waiting until she
was old enough to be married off. So that at the
years when one would hope that they would be really
responsive they were often shut in. Then of course it
was extremely difficult to visit them in their homes.
Simply because there is no privacy. Often there were

several families sharing in one house and there were always interruptions.

There didn't appear to be any religious instruction given to women and girls. One scarcely imagines that Muhammad thought that women and girls had souls because the Koran deals only with men. When we inquired about this, they would reply, "Well, we're donkeys; we don't understand anything; we're not told anything." Their only religious outlet it seems was visiting the saint's tomb. Whatever the trouble was in the family — a child or husband sick, a woman who was childless, etc. — their recourse was a visit to different saints' tombs. Also the only holiday the family had in the summer was usually to make a pilgrimage to the saint's tomb. Mother and children would all go together for a week or so taking their provisions and bedding and making a real holiday of it.

One of our great joys in those early days was to make trips, day trips that is, into the country to visit the bedouin women in their tents. These country women were always much easier to get at — once you passed the fierce dogs that guarded their encampment. But at least they were not veiled and they were not shut in. In my childhood days the trips were made on donkey back, but later in my early missionary days we began to know such luxuries as a little car; often a secondhand one which stood much hard work. But we were able to visit these ignorant country folk who were always very warm and very friendly. We often wondered how much they took in because it was always something completely new to them. But we could only leave the seed sown by the Spirit of God Who would take the small seed and cause it to germinate according to His eternal purposes and grace.

Then for a long period of time during the war years and for family reasons I was home in England. When I went back to Tunisia again the country had just

regained its independence. And what a change! The
French were gone, Tunisia had gained its independence and their president, Habib Bourghiba, was a
very enlightened man with advanced thoughts.

But the greatest change I found was in the state of
women. President Bourghiba, who had studied law
in France and had seen the freedom of western
women and the part they could play in national life,
had completely opened all the schools and determined that education should be free for all women.

He also urged them to throw aside their veils and
take their places in the national life; he even gave
women the right to vote. I think this was a bit of
good policy on his part because that put all the
women on his side.

But the big thing was seeing all the girls coming
out to school trotting along with their schoolbags
wanting to read and write on the same footing as the
boys. Of course there were not enough schools to go
around and there were not enough teachers either.
But there it was!

More than that, some of them were able to go on to
secondary education and even to university. They
sat side by side with male students and went on to
higher subjects. And others were going out to work
at hospitals and offices and teaching. But the great
transformation was in the opening of their minds.
They were no longer accepting things blindly as they
had done before. They were beginning to question
and to think.

And the first thing they thought about seriously
was their commitment to Islam. Before they had
been Muslims simply because they were told that
they were Muslims and that was that! But now they
began to want to know about their own faith. And of
course in school they were given regular Koranic
instruction. They learned to pray and you'd often go
in a home and you'd see girls who had never themselves been to school, older girls, who were neverthe-

less learning their prayers and religiously saying
their prayers at the stated time.

Then came the sudden reaction. As they went on
to higher education there was a turning to materialism. They began to want all the western things
western girls were having and earning money they
began to think of things like dress, hairstyles and
gradually their early religious fervor cooled off. They
became obsessed with the "good things" of this life.
Of course, a girl was not still completely free, even a
girl who went out to work. She still had to live at
home and hand over her money to her father who
would graciously hand her back some of it for her
own use.

But the greatest joy of all to me was that these
girls were now able to read the Scriptures for themselves. During my later years in Tunis we were
brought in contact with a number of secondary and
high school girls who began to come to our house.
We ran a sort of Friday afternoon girl's club. They
would come to our house and we would have discus-
sions and games and perhaps do needlework—
whatever they were interested in—and then settle
down to an hour of Bible study: reading Arabic
Scriptures, singing Arabic hymns, discussing Christianity with them.

The amazing thing was that the parents allowed
them to come. But the fact was, of course, that the
parents knew and trusted us. They knew they were
coming to us and they knew we were talking about
religion, but as I had one father say to me, "I trust
my girls with you but I wouldn't trust them to any
Muslim. I wouldn't even let them go to my neighbors." And the girls themselves were glad to come
because they felt we could understand them and
their lives in a way that their mothers couldn't. The
mothers had grown up in such a completely shut-in
atmosphere. With us they could discuss their studies
and problems and we could understand. It was a

great joy to be able to talk completely freely with
these girls.

But when some of them began to study French
and come in contact with teachings completely con-
trary to their Muslim faith they were seriously upset.
They began to read the writings of people who did
not believe in the existence of God at all. They came
in contact with teachers, some of whom were perhaps
communists, and the whole turmoil then took place
in their minds. These girls would argue among
themselves at night for hours. What was the truth?
Their minds were in complete turmoil.

They more or less took one of three paths; some of
them clung faithfully to their Muslim faith and belief
in God, others flung it all over and became openly
communistic, and others just let the whole thing
drop and became purely materialistic. But again it
was a great joy when these girls came sometimes to
us with these problems.

Perhaps I can best illustrate all this by telling a
story about a girl I once knew when we were living in
the little seaport town of Nabuel. I got in touch with
her when she was about thirteen. She lived a completely shut-in life; she lived with her mother and in
the morning they did the household chores together.
In the afternoon she would spend the whole day
sitting in the little entry; (the front door was open,
but there was a big curtain hanging down over the
front door, which looked out on the little alley where
they lived) she spent the whole afternoon sitting
crosslegged on the floor working on her embroidery
frame making a trousseau for her marriage. I used to
go about once a week to see this girl and would tell
her Bible stories. She was a very intelligent girl and
it was a joy to visit her. I went practically all
through the Bible with her.

I remember the horror that she and her mother
experienced when one of the older brothers who was
in high school in Tunis came back and began loftily

speaking about the fact that his professor said that
there was no God. But that was what he was
learning. You can scarcely imagine the horror it was
to that poor mother. Later this girl was married to a
man she had never seen and I went to her wedding.
Then the war intervened and she dropped out of my
life.

Years later when I came back I tried to hunt her
up again. I was directed to a house where I was told
she was living. The "girl" whom I had known before,
now a wife and mother, was out and I was received
by her daughter, a very pretty young girl in her
teens. She was dressed in western dress, and received
me quite charmingly. She served coffee in a nice
western drawing room and, speaking beautiful
French, told me that she was at boarding school at
Sousse and only came back home for the holidays.

I said to her, "Don't you girls sometimes in your
dormitories think about spiritual things—think
about God and eternal things?"

She said, "We do, but we're in a complete fog; we
don't know what to think."

That girl went on to university and married a
student she met there. Of course that created a great
upset in the family; she was going with a young man
that they had never met. He went to see her parents
in the proper fashion and asked for her hand in
marriage. As far as I know she was married and
settled down to a purely secular life.

But the great thing is that here are young people
ready and ripe for the Gospel message if only we
could get it to them. All kinds of other subversive
teachings are coming in, especially communism, and
the deadening influence of materialism. How important it is to get the truth of God from the Bible to
these open minds.

SUPPORT POLICY AND PROBLEMS

Financial support is an obvious and necessary part of the missionary program. The manner in which it is maintained, however, varies with the different character of the organizations—denominational or interdenominational—and the interpretation of Scriptural principles in each organization. Some missions never mention money matters at all; really. Some talk so much about not mentioning money that they actually bring their need of funds more forcefully to the attention of the public than if they had said nothing. Others use almost every technique and ploy of secular fundraising imaginable, leaning heavily on heart-wrenching stories and pathetic pictures. Most, however, simply "ask God and tell people" in a frank and honest report of facts without any pressure whatever.

Personally, I feel I have as much right to ask God's people for money to support His work as I have to ask for prayer. Or, put another way, I do not feel I have any more right to ask for prayer than I have to ask for money. If the work I represent is being conducted in a manner pleasing to God, it deserves the support of God's people as He directs. My part is to tell of the need for personnel and funds to do the work on the one hand, and the need for prayer to supply spiritual power, protection, blessing and material need to enable the doing of the work on the other. I ask for prayer and money. The frequent statements in the British magazine from the beginning against "solicitation" cannot refer to simply mentioning financial needs but rather to certain objectionable methods sometimes employed in order to press people to respond. Hardly an issue of the magazine appeared without notices to the effect that funds were low. In fact, often specific sums were mentioned. And the readers were asked not only to pray but give as much as they could in order to relieve emergencies, So there does not seem to be any real difference in practise then from the procedure I advocate now.

It seems to me the conflict or controversy over asking for prayer as against asking for money springs from the diverse nature of the two things in question. One, prayer, is intangible. The other, money, is tangible. Let me explain what I mean. If I should ask a person pointedly or directly for prayer, chances are he will consent; at least tacitly. In a sense it does not cost anything to do so. For even if he never does get around to praying, I will never know. With money, however, the situation is quite different. If I ask as pointedly or directly for money, a verbal response is not sufficient. My friend must either give or not as he chooses and his action in this connection is his real answer. It is not so embarrassing to ask for or to be asked by someone for prayer. No matter what the verbal response the one asking will rarely ever know the true answer. But to be confronted by a friend with a flat request for money is embarrassing especially if you do not feel able or inclined to give. Frankly, I believe we ought to be much more restrained in asking for prayer and much more candid in asking for money. Above all, be honest. Do not say, "Will you pray about my new car, or radio, or allowance," when you really mean "give." If you mean "pray," say "pray." If you mean "give," say "give." Maybe we ought only to ask people to pray about whether they should give.

In any case, there is a basic, fundamental difference in the funding of a denominational mission and an interdenominational one. So much so that the latter is frequently known as a "faith" mission. Although there is serious question whether the determination of "faith" depends solely upon denominational affiliation or lack of it. I suppose the fact that normally a denominational missionary society can expect the support of its constituent members whereas the interdenominational mission does not have a built-in constituency and must depend on the voluntary gifts of churches and individuals suggests the necessity for a greater exercise of faith in the latter case. As a matter of fact, however, there is a great deal more to faith than just receiving funds and the correct designation of a mission as a "faith" mission, it seems to me, surely ought to include not only the theological basis of the mission and the manner in which the work is carried out, but also the character of the personal spiritual lives of its members. Faith relates to more than fundraising.

In any case, the NAM was and is an interdenominational mission and therefore has always depended upon voluntary contributions. In fact, the first donation was the 100 pounds Guinness gave to Pearse before the founding trip in 1881. Apparently, there was no explicit written policy regarding finances in the early days. I suppose that for the first few years with only a few missionaries sustained by the initial enthusiasm of a new work funds were adequate. Indeed, the cost per missionary at this time was incredibly low. In 1886 it was only 80 pounds for a man and 60 pounds for a woman per year! This reminds me of the allowance figure set at the beginning of the work by the American Council. Counting on the fact that field properties were already owned or leased by the Mission with no provision for furlough travel or health care, we calculated in 1949, and for several years thereafter, that $75 a month was adequate support. Time is a great teacher.

By 1897 the figure in Britain had risen to 95 pounds and 75 pounds respectively for men and women. And by 1900 it was 120 and 100 respectively. Incidentally, by 1890 it had become painfully clear that travel was expensive and gifts for allowance would not cover furlough travel, so it was suggested that perhaps some folks would like to make special gifts of from 20 to 25 pounds for this purpose.

I find a suggestion of great interest in the magazine *North Africa* for 1886, repeated later in 1908, regarding the personal support of missionaries. After setting forth the figures for support it was noted that "the cost of living in Algeria and Tunisia is probably one-fourth more than in England and there are ten single ladies and four single men." Then we read, "Any person desiring to support one of the missionaries can choose one whom they can look upon as their representative." Another way this system worked is illustrated by the example of Mr. George Chapman in 1907. While working at the YMCA in Harrowgate, Mr. Chapman felt that God wanted him to serve with the NAM in Africa. As he prepared to go several of his friends at Harrowgate formed an Auxiliary of NAM there to care for his regular support besides providing for the cost of his outfit and passage.

I firmly believe that this practise of individuals or families at home assuming full support for a missionary—or as nearly full as possible—is the most practical and meaningful principle in financing the whole missionary enterprise. Pray for many different missions and missionaries, to be sure, for a wider perspective. But get involved personally by focusing or concentrating your interest and attention upon a few; and these in personal detail. Do not be a spectator from a distance, get involved personally through current information of one station or work in detail. You will understand and appreciate the real workings of missionary activity; the problems and solutions, the sorrows and joys, the pressures and advances, by intimate knowledge of one family and personally sharing with them. Missionary work everywhere will be far more meaningful to the degree that you are really a part of the work somewhere. This has been my constant emphasis ever since I began my work with NAM nearly thirty years ago. And I thought the idea was original with me!

From the start there were three categories of missionaries in NAM as far as support was concerned; first, some supported themselves entirely from private or family means; second, others were supported by gifts from friends or churches which sometimes were channeled to the Mission offices and sometimes were sent directly to the missionary; third, yet others were dependent for support upon the funds available to the Mission as a result of gifts and legacies to the General Fund. This system has the disadvantage of preventing a systematic distribution of necessary monies to all missionaries from one central source. The Mission never knows whether or not the need of all its missionaries are being met. Although I strongly suspect that the missionaries supporting themselves or supported by personally designated gifts were better and more regularly supported than the other (for the reasons stated above relating to the benefit of personal links with missionaries). What is everybody's responsibility is nobody's responsibility and frequently does not get done by anybody.

In his valedictory message to the International Council in 1975, Mr. Stalley then retiring from 24 years service with NAM, made a strong plea for the exercise of a responsible attitude toward the missionaries on the part of the Council and friends at home. He warned against the danger that a "faith principle" requiring the missionaries to recognise that their total dependence is upon God can become a cover for irresponsibility on the part of the people at home. He added, "I am convinced that any progress in recruiting missionaries must go hand in hand with the recruiting of others who will accept responsibility for them."

The North American office has always operated on the basis of designated gifts to individual missionaries put into a central pool from which all missionaries receive their allowances and expenses. However, this was not so much a matter of policy in the beginning as it was a matter of necessity. When the American Council had been in operation less than a year and had total assets of less than $500, a young couple applied for service. As there was no General Fund capable of sending them out they sought and found God's appointed servants to undertake their support. No obligation was involved. Only an intention was declared; as God enables. Certainly this does not conflict with the Mission's policy statement as historically declared, "No salary (is) guaranteed by the Mission to the missionaries, their trust must be directly in God for the supply of all their needs."

It is plain, therefore, that no matter what the mechanics employed ultimately all our needs—and surely that includes spiritual as well as physical—are supplied by God. On the other hand, we, as officers, are responsible under God's direction to do our part in seeing that those needs are indeed supplied. So there are important decisions facing us; what steps should we take to open channels for support, how shall we handle gifts as they come in, what shall we do in cases of shortages of funds, etc. The most important thing is to be sure that the plans laid and the decisions taken are really in accordance with God's will for us. Humanly speaking, this is a highly subjective area in which it is easy to follow our own inclinations or desires rather than God's direction. It is all very well to remind ourselves that "God's work done God's way will never fail of God's supply." But that does not mean that God will never, for His purposes, bring times of straitening. However, it must surely mean that our faithful obedience to His will insures reasonably adequate and regular supplies so that His work not be seriously hindered. Whatever the means if they be God's choice, His work will prosper.

But now let us turn to a very practical consideration; what happens if funds run short while new applicants are at hand? Is it exercising faith to send new recruits out when there are insufficient funds to pay the allowances of missionaries already on the field? This is precisely the question that was faced in an article in the August 1890 issue of *North Africa* in the following words. "People sometimes say, 'Do you think that it is right to send out more workers when those in the field are only receiving very slender supplies for their personal needs, and would gladly have more also for the expenses of the work?' To this we reply that we only desire to do God's will, and send out those whom He is calling. 'Them that honor Me I will honor.' "

Brave words, implying that to hesitate is to lack faith while to push ahead is exercising faith. However, in the March number of *The Reaper* that same year, Mr. John Anderson, founder of the Southern Morocco Mission writes, "A number of young men and women, several of whom are receiving a medical training, have offered for service in connection with the mission, and we are hopeful that the Lord may open the way and enable us to accept them. We now plainly say that one necessary condition is that sufficient funds be sent in for their support. If God means us to extend this work, He will send the needed resources." It is not clear whether the policy of NAM was ever explicitly and formally changed. But the record does show than on several occasions after 1890, new workers were indeed held back when funds were low until there was sufficient money first of all to make up arrears in allowances, then to send out the new workers.*

But the amazing thing is that in spite of recurrent periods of financial shortage, and there is frequent notice to that effect again and again in the magazine, the work kept on. There was never a sense of panic or desperation. The situation was faced as a temporary testing period. It was expected that a faithful Heavenly Father would bring relief. On one occasion special thanks to God was recorded when after an unusually dry period followed by a stated day of prayer, three times the needed sum was received in a few days.

There was, to be sure, one time when things did look rather grim. With the close of World War II a period of general

* c.f. e.g. North Africa, *1907, p. 53; 1921, p. 12; 1931, 86.*

economic upset in Europe had dire effect in North Africa. Prices
for everyday commodities had more than tripled during the war
and the purchasing power of English money in North Africa
was further diminished by being pegged at 200 fr. to the pound.
The result was that a night watchman earned twice what a
missionary received and "the price for soling and heeling a pair
of shoes in Tunis cost 3 pounds!" But when the franc was
devalued to 480 to the pound, there was considerable relief.
However, a little over a year later another crisis developed.
Stated succinctly in a magazine report, "For the second time
this year . . . we were unable to send out the usual monthly
allowance to our workers . . . our coffers are empty . . . far from
being able to accept new recruits, we may even be compelled to
reduce our forces."

Once again God supplied in answer to fervent prayer. The
financial position was strengthened and in the following year
several new workers went out to fill vacancies left by the losses
sustained through the war. It was at that point that God led the
British Council to expand the base of the Mission by reviving
the Auxiliary Councils in North America.

Once a Field Administration was set up with a Field Treasurer the amount of missionary allowances and contributions to a
common fund for general field expenses was determined on the
field by the Field Treasurer and applied to all missionaries
irrespective of their home countries. Additional sums to care for
home expenses (furlough, medical, etc.) are the responsibility of
the respective Home Councils. How these monies are acquired
is the province of each Home Council. There have been occasions when one Home Council has helped another which was
experiencing a period of financial stress which is another
exercise in Christian grace between members of one family.

Shortage of funds to support legitimate works of God
overseas is the result of spiritual default. Therefore, it must be
dealt with as a spiritual problem. It is after all a matter of
spiritual cooperation between Christians at home and missionaries overseas. If the Mission gains the confidence of the
churches at home, it has the right to expect their support in
prayer and finances. Both missions and churches should expect
God to lead them into partnership relations wherein by disci-

pline and sacrifice they can pursue the work of worldwide
evangelization and church planting for His glory.

MEDICAL WORK

One of the most successful means of introducing the Gospel
message to non-Christian peoples in undeveloped areas of the
world, medical ministries, have often been at the forefront of
missionary programs. It is possible by meeting dire physical
needs to demonstrate to the host population not only a real
personal concern for those needs but also a willingness to do
something about them. Thus prejudices are broken down and
acceptance is won for the strange foreign guest and sometimes
also a hearing for the message the guest brings with him.

Therefore, from the beginning, some type of medical ministry
played an important part in the work of the North Africa
Mission. Even at the first station, Djemaa Sahridj, in the hills
of Kabylia, a simple dispensary functioned as part of the work
although French law virtually prohibited medical practice by
those not licensed by French authorities.

When missionaries entered Morocco in 1883 they found a
country plagued by numerous diseases with no hygienic program or controls and not a single hospital. The first property
purchased had been the home of a retired Englishman and bore
the name "Bleak House," doubtless derived from the name of a
popular novel by Charles Dickens. However, it was decided that
the name "Hope House" was more appropriate for a Christian
residence, so the change was effected. The following year Mr. E.
F. Baldwin from America with his wife and five daughters
joined the Mission and assumed leadership of the newly started
Moroccan outpost. As Mrs. Baldwin's father was a doctor she
had some acquaintance with medical work, so she set up a
dispensary in their home. In 1885 a qualified man, Dr. T. G.
Churcher, was secured and went out to Tangier to strengthen
the medical ministry. Miss Hughina Tulloch went out the same
year and joined the Baldwin family. She helped with the
children while studying Arabic. Miss Tulloch had come from a
strong Christian family in Scotland, was early converted and
immediately engaged in Christian witness. She also had had

unusual opportunities for education in Edinburgh and Frank-
furt-am-Main, Germany and was an exceptional linguist. In
addition to taking care of the Baldwin children she also helped
Dr. Churcher with his patients while they waited for treatment.
Within the year several of the missionaries went down with
typhoid including Miss Tulloch. Weakened by an earlier illness
and in spite of every possible care she died December 11, 1886,
the first casualty to illness among the scores of missionaries
who would later be lost by this means.* So when a dilapidated
Moorish stable adjacent to Hope House was later purchased
and remodelled to become the first hospital not only of the
Mission but of any kind in the entire country of Morocco it was
named the Tulloch Memorial Hospital in her memory.

This hospital was put into shape by Dr. T. G. Churcher
1887-1888 and was equipped for twenty inpatient beds and an
outpatient clinic with a small operating theatre. In 1938 a new
wing was attached for outpatients, radiology, dispensary and
modern doctor's office and examination room. Its ministry
continued until finally the whole property including Hope
House was expropriated by the Moroccan government in 1974.
For some years, just before expropriation, plans were being
considered for a major remodelling of the older building at a
projected cost of about 10,000 pounds. But as time went on it
was thought wise to delay this plan since the future of the
institutional missionary ministries seemed less than certain.
Anyway, by this time there were several large hospitals in
Morocco including one quite close to TMH and medical schools
as well.

It is likely that the whole Marshan complex at Tangier,
including not only Hope House and TMH but also a small
chapel and three residences, was occupied more continuously
than any other station in North Africa. It served as a focus for
several different ministries. Moreover, the influence of the
hospital spread far wider than its modest accommodations
might suggest. Frequent visits to villages all over northern
Morocco followed up patients who had come for treatment to
Tangier. Often villages just off the main road south, which
missionaries longed to visit but which were guarded by vicious
dogs and stubborn people, opened up when a member of the

---

* *In fact, within seven years [between 1906 and 1913] two doctors [Roberts
and Wilson] and two nurses [Ida and Georgina Smith, sisters] died of Typhus
and associated diseases.*

village was taken for treatment to the hospital. Again the
trouble was that far more villages began requesting visits from
the Tabib (doctor) and his associates than the limited staff
could accommodate.

In fact because of limited facilities and personnel it was
necessary to limit admissions for the most part to surgical
cases. To be sure, in 1954 two T.B. wards were created in the
newer section of the hospital. But it was important for the staff
to bear in mind the primary purpose of the hospital and that
was evangelism.

Because eye problems (cataracts and trichiases) were so
prevalent and surgical correction so simple yet dramatic it was
decided to concentrate on them. Dr. Farnham St. John, who
went out in 1945 to take over during a difficult time of
transition, later returned to England for additional training in
eye surgery to equip himself for this specialty. Dr. William F.
Campbell from Ohio, U.S.A. went out as a general surgeon in
1955. Later he took a post as a private physician in Safi until
expelled by the government. Both men as real missionary
doctors were fluent in the language and apt in teaching the
Word. They realized that the person who has experienced
physical relief at the hands of the doctor is more open to him for
a spiritual ministry than to a professional "hospital evangelist."

In order to understand better the way of village visitation let
us hear from Tabib St. John in his own words.

> Sometimes a case in a more distant village gives
> an opportunity of preaching in a hitherto unreached
> place. One Sunday afternoon in December, 1949, an
> old man came to the hospital and asked me to go and
> see his daughter who was "very, very ill" in a village
> about ten miles away. All patients on Sundays or at
> night are thus described lest there should be delay in
> their being visited, but I felt, as is usually the case,
> that it was best to go and investigate and see if we
> could reach the house in the car. I found her shortly
> after sunset in a hut in the middle of the village, and
> his description of her was fully justified. She was

eighteen years old, but had it not been for an
enormous intra-abdominal abscess, I could have
lifted her up with one hand. As my eyes grew
accustomed to the gloom I saw that her limbs were
like sticks, her face white and drawn, and her voice
was almost inaudible.

"How long have you been ill, Habeeba?"

"About three Fridays."

"How did it start?"

"God sent it."

"Yes, but what else happened?"

"I had a baby, but it's dead."

"Will you come to the hospital?"

"Yes, that is why I sent for you."

She was a divorced girl, and so there was no
mother-in-law to be argued with, and we set out at
once.

The journey to the hospital must have tortured
her, as the car was running in the dark over ploughed
field and low scrub. After a few miles we had to stop
to change a wheel, and the rest did her good. She was
still alive when we reached Tangier, and Sister soon
made her comfortable. It was Christmas Eve, and
everyone was busy, but Habeeba had priority. Next
morning we were able to assess her clinical condition
more accurately, and the picture really seemed hopeless. The abscess burst her abdomen and closure was
impossible, as the anterior abdominal wall on that
side no longer existed. A terrible cough made it
difficult to control the wound. Next day further
complications developed and it seemed impossible
that she could survive. However, Habeeba was a
fighter, and so was Sister, and their combined tena-
city and courage and two wonderful synergic therapeutic measures, prayer and penicillin, won the day.
She got no worse, and as the weeks passed we
realised with wonder that she was going to live.
Three months later, she went home on her father's
donkey, and we wondered whether the villagers

would know her, so much had her appearance altered.

Before returning to England, we went out to visit her. We had a great welcome in the village and a tea-party was arranged in her home. Neighbors came in, and when tea was over Mr. Cooper explained to them why we had come to their land and what God, Who had healed their Habeeba, wanted to do. "He can heal bodies; He can heal hearts." I thought of our Lord's words when He drove home His message of forgiveness by healing the body of the paralytic. "Whether it is easier to say to the sick of the palsy, 'Thy sins be forgiven thee,' or to say, 'Arise, and take up thy bed and walk.' But that ye may know that the Son of Man hath power on earth to forgive sins (He saith to the sick of the palsy), I say unto thee, 'Arise, and take up thy bed and go thy way into thine house,' " I do not think that Habeeba has yet received the forgiveness of sins, but I know that through her healing many were amazed and glorified God as of old. They gave an attentive hearing to the message of salvation.

"There's only one more river to cross," said our guide, as we all climbed out of the car and started to push it out of the mud, where its back wheels were firmly stuck. Only one more river bed, but about five more miles of waste, undulating land. There was no road, but our guide, a black-bearded Moor, kept pointing eagerly ahead; for somewhere among these low hills there nestled a village, and in that village was a hut, where a woman lay on the floor desperately ill.

With a final tremendous bump we topped the last rise, and the village lay in the hollow below us, shimmering in the heat—a collection of thatched bamboo huts surrounded by a hedge of prickly pear cactus. Every child and every dog in the settlement had come out to meet us but at the sight of a motor the younger children gathered up their long skirts and scattered in all directions, shrieking with terror and delight.

"My wife is in here," said our guide, and we stooped down and followed him through the low entrance to where in the semi-darkness a youngish woman lay on a rush mat. Her six children hung around the door—beautiful, shy, dark-eyed children, smiling up into the face of the doctor.

The woman had nephritis. The husband would come back with us in the car, fetch the medicine and walk the twelve miles back as he had walked the twelve miles to fetch us.

Out into the sunshine, to find that the village had collected outside. A crowd of men, smiling and friendly, squatted in the shade of the thatch. The women stood at a little distance staring, and the children caught hold of our hands and pressed around us.

So, for half an hour we squatted with them. They were shepherds and tillers of the soil, and we read them the story of the Lost Sheep. When the sheep was found they threw back their heads and laughed.

"Can you read?" asked the doctor when he had explained the story. They laughed again at the very idea.

"No, no, none of us can read—we are like the beasts. Come again and tell us another story out of your book."

"Yes, come again, come again!" cried the children, clustering round the motor and rushing squealing up the hill as the engine started.

But we have never been again. There are so many little villages, nestling among the hills, so many sick in the big slums of the city, so many thronging the doors of the little hospital—and so few to go to them.

Even when government facilities began to appear as the Moroccan Department of Health extended its services ever more widely through the country, many Moroccans preferred to take their relatives to TMH. The equipment in the government hospitals was superior to that in TMH but compassionate nursing care was rare. And the evident loving care of the Christian staff at TMH had no counterpart whatsoever in the other institutions.

One time the son of a Tangier policeman was taken to the local government hospital. He had fallen from the second floor of his house to the courtyard below and was unconscious. When his father heard where his son was he went immediately and insisted that the boy be transferred to TMH. The hospital authorities refused his request so he simply went into the ward where his son was, picked up the boy and carried him out of the hospital and up the street to TMH. His explanation to the missionaries was simple and to the point, "I don't know much about the science of medicine, but I know you will take more loving care of my son." The unselfish, sacrificial attention of the foreign medical specialists for even the simplest village or country folk confirmed the message of Divine love they shared with their patients at every opportunity. In fact the popular name among the Tangier population for TMH was "The House of God."

Frequently medical miracles occurred in response to what was known as "those two wonderful, synergic, therapeutic measures, prayer and penicillin." Though often it was simply correct and untiring loving care combining mind and heart which carried seemingly impossible cases through to restored health. And so it was also on all the medical stations where either midwives ministered in the homes or general missionaries provided simple remedies for the ever present ills of the people.

From 1954 on there was a short course nurses training program which attracted girls from all over Morocco and even Algeria. Miss Patricia St. John (sister of Dr. Farnham St. John) was the founder and director of this work. The purpose was to give simple medical training, especially midwifery, to North African Christian girls so they could help meet the pressing medical needs of their homelands while maintaining a Christian witness. Since in the development of Moroccan medical services, there were far more doctors than nurses and

qualified nursing care is still relatively rare, there was a real
place of service for such persons. These TMH nursing trainees
had to complete their studies abroad for complete qualification.
Most of them went to England since their training at TMH had
been in English. Unfortunately not all who went to England
returned to Morocco. Many, however, have taken jobs in
government hospitals in Morocco.

A few years after the TMH got started plans were made to
extend a special inpatient service for women in the Tangier
area. So in 1894 Dr. Terry, successor to Dr. Churcher at TMH,
secured a private house in the city with six beds and space also
for outpatients as a special facility for Moroccan women.
Shortly thereafter Dr. Gabrielle Breeze took charge. After only
a few years this operation had to be moved to a smaller house
on the Marshan and thereafter it could be run only as a
dispensary. After twenty-five years, at Dr. Breeze's death, the
work ceased.

Another small hospital was run by Dr. Grieve in Casablanca
for about fifteen years. But after the property was destroyed
during a bombardment of the city in 1907, it too ceased
operation. These hospitals were supplemented by small dispensaries and the services of midwives in several of the large cities
of Morocco, principally Fes, Tetuan, Larash, Marrakech, and
for short periods in Ouezzane, Alkazar, Chauen, Safi, and El
Jadida.

When after independence the Moroccan Government declined
to recognize the legal status of the Mission all institutional
work in the name of NAM had to stop. Moreover, new
missionaries had to get some type of employment as individuals
in order to secure resident permits. Still medical services were
found to be useful and so NAM medical personnel got positions
as, for example, private physician, supervisor of private clinic,
office nurse, midwife, etc. So medical practice is still useful for
the missionary witness in Morocco.

Outside Morocco medical work never played a major role for
long. In fact, French regulations strictly limited any medical
services in Algeria. In Tunisia, from time to time dispensaries
in Tunis, Sousse and Sfax were operated often with the service
of a doctor, but there was never a hospital.

Tripoli, on the other hand, the only station ever occupied in Libya, was always chiefly a medical outpost. After Mr. Reid had for many years borne a faithful witness from the dispensary there, he was followed by Dr. James Liley and he in turn was succeeded at retirement by Dr. Patrick McCarthy, until all missionary work was terminated in 1969.

When regular permission to function ceased in 1960 Dr. McCarthy and his wife went to Egypt intending to obtain Libyan visas so he could practice as a private physician. After ten weeks of waiting they got their visas and returned to Tripoli. However, nine years later while on furlough they were strongly advised not to return because the situation had seriously deteriorated, so all NAM work in Libya ended.

Now that missionaries must have jobs to work in North Africa (see *Special Service Workers*, Chapter IV, page 77) some form of medical service might provide an opportunity to resume a Christian witness in Libya.

INDUSTRIAL WORK

Over the years the Mission has employed various kinds of industrial work in order to attract and hold North Africans for continuous or intensive exposure to the Gospel and systematic teaching in the Christian life. These programs never assumed great proportions and as far as making for continuing groups of Christians they have been of doubtful value. Certainly many children and adults were converted over the years through the Bible teaching involved, but when the missionaries left or the work had to be closed down the national Christian group shrank to almost nothing.

On a small scale many missionaries have developed classes in various handcrafts to maintain regular attendance. For example, missionary women taught children and girls knitting, sewing, embroidery and even rugmaking; often combined with reading and writing where possible. Doubtless thousands of North Africans have become true and knowledgeable Christians as a result of such systematic teaching. But the vast majority of the girls as they grew up were married to Muslim husbands and have been completely lost to sight. It is unbelievably hard to maintain a vital Christian life when both cut off from fellowship with other Christians and also virtually buried under the pressure of the Muslim religion and culture. However, now and then an apparently new person will venture to a Christian meeting and show unusual knowledge of the Gospel for a stranger. Upon close questioning it turns out that many years before as a child the newcomer attended classes at a mission house and many of the stories, verses and songs learned long ago are still remembered. So though outward results are often not impressive, nevertheless, the seed sown often does spring up into life.

One farm and home for men and boys founded in Tangier by Mr. Jeremiah Edwards in 1897 eventually became the Raymond Lull Orphanage operated by an independent Canadian missionary, Mr. Herbert Elson. Mr. Edwards bought a property on the mountain just outside Tangier and planned a farm with fruit trees, vines and livestock to be operated by men together with a home for boys. When he resigned from NAM in 1902, Mr. Elson bought the property. The farming side ceased but the boys home became an orphanage which produced several boys who later became Christian men in the community. Years later another farming project started in northern Morocco, this time in Tetuan. For a while it was combined with a project to teach a couple of Christian men silk screen printing. But neither project lasted very long. The purpose of the farm was to provide a healthy refuge for Tangier boys who had had some contact with the Gospel, but in Tangier were living in so sinful an environment of drugs, immorality and thievery they had little chance to respond positively to the Christian message. Unfortunately, however, they had already been so seriously affected by their environment they were disinclined either to work or study.

The single largest and most impressive industrial project of the NAM was the Cherchell Carpet School in Algeria. Opened by Miss Helena Day in 1903 it soon comprised eight large looms for knotting mats, rugs and carpets (so designated according to size though made in the same fashion). First it was young girls and later women who were trained in this work. Part of the day was given to instruction in Bible, of course, for this was the main purpose of the work. However, it also gave many women gainful employment since the rugs were shipped to England for sale. A brochure inserted in the magazine for November 1911 lists fifty-four items for sale ranging from a mat 22 inches x 10 inches for two shillings to a carpet 14 feet 6 inches x 9 feet three inches for 13 pounds, 10 shillings (more than a missionary's monthly allowance!). This work ceased during the period of unrest accompanying World War II.

One small industrial project in Algeria made an interesting impact on the local culture. In 1918 Mr. Thomas Warren introduced an unusual type of woodcarving from England into the village of Djemaa Sahridj, Algeria. Several of his apprentices became quite skillful at it and the trade caught on. In 1924 when Mr. Warren was transferred to Paris he sold his equipment to the Methodist missionaries who continued the training. This distinctive style of woodcarving done in the Kabyle hills is still very popular and is widely thought to be a native Berber craft.

Today, of course, it would be difficult if not impossible, to conduct an independent Mission industrial project. All business enterprises are strictly controlled by the governments and any direct relationship to Christian activity would probably be prohibited. Missionaries engaged in business of one kind or another do so in order to maintain themselves in their respective countries for personal witness, not to conduct Christian training alongside the business.

WORLD WAR II

Suddenly, war broke out. The apprehensive years of negotiations with the increasingly belligerent German government by an overly optimistic British Prime Minister terminated with the Wehrmacht's invasion of Poland. After a short stalemate as the opposing armies of France and Germany glared at one another from their respective fortifications in the Maginot and Siegfried Lines, the German forces burst through, swept all opposition before them clear to the English Channel and Marshal Petain assumed control of a defeated France from Vichy.

The big questions were, how much further will this go and

how will it affect missions in North Africa. Two important
factors bearing on the answers to these questions were the
extent to which Vichy control of the North African countries
would limit or even prohibit missionary activity and to what
degree travel and financial restrictions in Britain would force
reduction or even termination of the NAM ministry.

As it turned out, the situation did not deteriorate drastically.
To be sure, travel to and from North Africa became more
difficult. There were long delays waiting for visas. Railroad
trips often took three or four times as long; the cost of furlough
travel increased by about a third; petrol became much more
expensive and scarce in supply; special permits were required
for travel outside the major cities in North Africa; there were
long lines at the shops for goods nearly always in short supply;
and, of course, rationing. But other than that life went on very
much as it had before the war began.

Communication, however, was a real problem. And mail from
Tangier to Britain was by far the fastest and most reliable. How
fortunate, then, that Mr. Thomas Warren, the Field Superintendent, had chosen to establish his office in Tangier just before
war broke out. He was able to collect information from the
missionaries across the field and channel it to Britain. He was
also able to receive funds for allowances from Britain and
dispatch them to the missionaries.

In connection with the question of continuing support for the
missionaries from Britain it was encouraging to hear from the
Foreign Secretary, Lord Halifax, of his expressed personal
concern. In a letter to Dr. W. Paton, Secretary of the International Missionary Council, Lord Halifax wrote, "As you know,
action already taken by several Government departments has
shown the desire of the British Government that the services
rendered by Christian missions should continue. I am myself
quite clear that the support of foreign missionary work in time
of war is an essential part of the Church's witness. I should
much regret if the responsibility which Christian people rightly
feel toward the special needs and charities that press upon us in
war-time should lead them to desert permanent and universal
Christian obligation." Well put; and reasonable. However, it
does require the exercise of special discipline for Christians to

remember that the claims of a present world-wide military conflict should not be allowed to obscure the prior claims of the larger and continuing spiritual warfare. If it is necessary to reduce personal expenses to meet the needs of the one, it may well be necessary to reduce them even further to meet the needs of the other. Apparently, that was done. Although there were periods of financial shortage of NAM funds from time to time—as usual—and sometimes delay in transmission, nevertheless, funds did come in and the work went on. In fact, new workers were received and sent out to the field.

The most trying period of service came near the close of the war in the European theatre when German forces moved into Tunisia. When Field Marshal Rommel's Afrika Korps was finally halted just short of Cairo and, after the battle of El Alamein, then driven back out of Egypt and Libya things became much tighter. Near the end of this time Operation Torch, the Allied landing in Morocco and Algeria, put Anglo-American forces into North Africa. These troops marched quickly eastward forcing the Germans (and their more or less unwilling allies, the Italians) to move north into Tunisia in order to establish a holding position, if possible, and, if not, at least secure a port for eventual evacuation. This brought war with the German armies into territory where missionary activity was going on. Up to this time the French had exercised only limited control on personal habits. Now restrictions were increased and many persons arrested and interned.

One NAM missionary in Tunis, Robert I. Brown, decided to keep right on at his work out of his home. Not long afterward he was arrested, sent to a POW camp in Germany by way of a camp in Italy and spent 18 months there. Food and clothing were scarce but he had books to study and as his profession became known and he was appointed Chaplain in his camp he had excellent opportunities for witness and Bible studies. In fact, he took courses by correspondence with the University of London leading to a B. A. in French and Arabic. So his time was hardly wasted.

Another missionary, R. Stanley Miles, elected to go into hiding. For a time this meant staying with first one Tunisian family after another for short periods. On one occasion German soldiers searched the house where he was in hiding but on reaching the top of the stairs and the very door of the room turned back and went downstairs again. Inside the fugitives were on their knees in prayer and felt "as though there were a wall of fire around them." After a while he decided not to jeopardize or involve his friends so he stayed in his own flat in the medina and ventured forth discreetly from time to time.

Mr. Stalley found a different situation in Algeria. He and his wife, Jess, with their young daughter were in Tlemcen when France fell. At first they were told they would be sent to a prison camp so they made arrangements with some friendly French people to take care of the baby. Then the order was countermanded and they were put under house arrest. This lasted for eighteen months and although food was scarce and funds often got so low that they all lost considerable weight, God wonderfully preserved them. Eventually, in November 1943, the American forces who landed in Oran liberated them and for a whole year after that Mr. Stalley served with the American Red Cross. This gave opportunities for hospitality and for witness to thousands of American soldiers. As Mr. Stalley puts it, "This was my first introduction to those wonderfully wild and friendly Americans and their extraordinary life style; good preparation for later years when North America joined in with the NAM." On two occasions after the American takeover in Algeria, Mr. Stalley met French officers in the city of Tlemcen who expressed genuine surprise to see him. One, a member of the former French Secret Service, said, "Why is it you are standing in front of me alive today?" "Why do you ask that?" replied Mr. Stalley. "My predecessor had decided to get rid of you. You were dangerous as a British spy," was the rejoinder. "Well, you see there was a higher hand over me and mine and that hand was God's," said Mr. Stalley. The officer simply shrugged his shoulders, "I wish I had your faith," he said. And so God preserved his servant who would serve as the first Field Director and later as International Secretary of the NAM for over twenty years.

4

EXPANSION: 1946—1980

"A NEW THING"

It is obvious that we have come to the end of an era in our Mission's history, an end that is as distinct as its beginning. That new departure took place in 1951. . . . The prospect was dim, the outlook unpromising. . . . There had been realists among missionaries even then who decided that the task was impossible and had given up. . . .

1951 saw the drawing up of an entirely new Constitution, a Home Council brought into being in the U.S.A. and another in Canada. The new structure had as an essential feature its field leadership in the hands of a Field Director living and operating on the field.

The majority of missionaries the Field Director (Mr. Stalley) was sent to lead were older than he. . . . It wasn't easy for the older ones to accept this young stranger who had landed in their midst; he hadn't even grown up amongst them!

A promise God gave me from the start to sustain faith was Isaiah 43:19, "Behold, I will do a *new thing*; now it shall spring forth; shall ye not know it?"

Now that era closes and another one opens. . . . It is marked by the departure of the appointee of 1951 from the field and also by the passing of the accepted, conventional missionary service of days gone by. . . . God is not tied to methods. He Himself does not change, neither does His purpose and Message. The record of the past twenty-four years is evidence of that.

Mr. Harold Stalley's report to
the International Council of 1975

HYMN

O Lord our God, whose lofty throne
The nations of the earth commands,
Thy sovereign power, we pray, make known
Throughout great Afric's northern lands.

Bid Egypt heed Thy voice once more,
And Libya hearken and obey;
Yea, speak until the utmost shore
Of Mauritania owns Thy sway.

Awake the conscience; give the sense
Of guilt and helplessness and loss,
Till through the tears of penitence
Men see the glory of the Cross.

Oh, thus on Afric's northern coast
Thy right maintain, Thy rule restore,
And Father, Son and Holy Ghost,
Shall have the praise for evermore.

Anon.

FROM INDEPENDENCE ON

As the years passed relations between missionary societies and the North African countries continued to deteriorate. Little by little the leaders of the independent Muslim states changed their attitude toward all foreign religions. In Tunisia, for example, many Roman Catholic churches and institutions were abruptly closed on the ground that since the European population was considerably reduced they were no longer needed. When in 1963, Tunisia rescinded the statutes of NAM over the successful operation of the Bible Correspondence Course there, concern arose in Mission circles that at some future date all missionaries might be expelled from North Africa. Perhaps Algeria would act next. But not Morocco, so it seemed, for the Moroccans appeared anxious to maintain good political and commercial relations with the West. As it turned out, however, the Moroccan government did crack down on missionary activity in 1967 and many missionaries were expelled. Nearly all of the Gospel Missionary Union personnel were forced out, although only a few of the NAM were affected. On the other hand, Algeria accepted the newly drafted statutes of NAM in 1975 in spite of earlier appearances of opposition. It was a short honeymoon, however, for two years later this order was rescinded and NAM no longer had any legal status in that country either. So plans were drawn up for the redeployment of expelled missionaries that would prevent their forced return to their homeland and possible loss to the Mission.

Southern France seemed a good place to go since the Radio School of the Bible was already located there. There were some temptations to get deeply involved in ministry to North Africans in Europe since it appeared that the conventional approach to missionary work would soon be no longer possible in North Africa itself. But as we studied the situation and prayerfully reexamined our original and continuing mandate to see the Church reestablished in North Africa we turned again in that direction and sought new ways to support the spread of the Gospel there. If worst came to worst, and it became impossible for missionaries to reside in North Africa, it was planned that teams of itinerant Bible teachers based outside the countries, but travelling in relays would be sent in to assist national Christians in their own spiritual lives as well as sharing in an expanded outreach. As things turned out, however, most of the NAM people were not summarily expelled. However, they experienced difficulty in renewing their residence permits, for the North African governments did not consider the category of missionary a valid reason for granting such permits. In fact, by Fall of 1978 even the French government made permanent residence (more than 3 months) much more difficult to obtain. It is now necessary to apply for a special visa in one's homeland before entering France.

The new relationship between the national governments and the Mission, however, did not halt or even deter the plans for the evangelization of North Africa. In fact, what at first appeared to be a serious setback actually turned out in some respects to be a step forward. When Field and RSB Headquarters had to be transferred across the Mediterranean to the south of France the chief result was a wider scope of ministry. More work could be done with no political restraint and travel to all points of North Africa was much facilitated. Perhaps it cost more; but that was a small price to pay for the distinct advantages to the ministry.

When it became clear that missionary status would no longer qualify one for a residence card in North Africa, some people concluded that missionary work had come to an end and the door was "closed." Others felt that the response to radio was so great and the moving of the Holy Spirit on lives so encouraging that there simply must be some way to continue the ministry. Over the years interest in the Muslim world has grown. More and more Christians in our homelands have joined in prayer for the revival of the Church in North Africa. Surely, we cannot give up now.

It was suggested that perhaps Christians could go singly into North Africa, not calling themselves missionaries and independent of mission organization. However, single volunteers rarely get sufficient language. Furthermore, their work suffers from the lack of coordination and direction which a Mission provides. They do indeed have some opportunities for witness but their service should be seen only as supplemental to, not a subsitute for, a more organized work.

There is another option which will probably become more and more popular and even spread to other countries as local governmental restrictions grow around the world. This is missionaries, in the commonly accepted sense, who can get jobs in the country of their appointment and on that basis acquire resident status. We call such people Special Service Workers although in fact they may soon consitute the general category of overseas workers as missionaries in the future. These SSW are screened by us as a Mission in the homeland for personal, biblical and spiritual maturity as well as Christian service experience and marketable skills. If found qualified, they are sent to overseas centers for orientation and linguistic training under the supervision of the Mission leaders and then they are posted with compatible colleagues in strategic locations to support the overall work of church planting. Such personnel go out with both prayer and financial support just like regular missionaries. They are linked with supporting churches at home and benefit from that association in every way. Although they will eventually get jobs and, of course, salaries, they still need financial support since for the first few years at least they will be without jobs while studying in the missionary training center. And even when the time comes to get a job it may be only a part-time one, allowing more time for the ministry. And in any case the salary will be relatively modest compared to the job situation at home so whatever extra money accrues from their employment can be used to further their own personal ministry, or assist a project related to it or else be applied to the other ministries of the Mission.

The underlying purpose of this scheme is to provide spiritually qualified, linguistically competent people who will be able to serve both as pioneers and partners in furthering the restoration of the Church in North Africa. There are many areas where pioneering is required. There are also scores of serious inquirers and new Christians who need much personal assistance through partnership. In most cases inquirers and new Christians are widely scattered so that contact with mature national Christians is nearly impossible. Furthermore, where small groups of national Christians are appearing they need partners to help them grapple with the painful problems of individual and

corporate growth. And the various aspects of Christian education and spiritual growth require different kinds of specially
trained people and materials which only an organized effort can
provide.

For a time after NAM lost its legal status the missionaries in
one country overreacted by terminating their coordinating
framework (Regional Superintendent and Regional Council)
and even questioning their right to be called missionaries at all,
especially when they got jobs which were listed on their
residence cards rather than the category of missionary. The
result was that lacking leadership teamwork broke down and
confusion spread. When the missionaries discovered that in
spite of appearances the government authorities actually knew
exactly who they were and what they were doing but were
satisfied with the situation since legally and technically they
were not listed as "missionaries," they realized that they could
carry on then privately if not officially in the eyes of the
Government as missionaries. They felt free to acknowledge
among themselves that they really were basically members of
the NAM and worked together with that understanding.

We are not deceiving the governments. We are meeting their
demands regarding the official dissolution of the statutes of the
NAM in North Africa and are fulfilling their requirements
regarding qualifications for residence cards. Let us not deceive
ourselves. We are not playing games with the North African
governments like "cops and robbers." They have complete
dossiers on everybody. We are able to continue in North Africa
not because we are clever or deceitful but because God wants us
there and has shown us how to adapt to the new conditions
which working under Islamic sovereignty has created. We must
be alert to the future. Further political developments might
curtail activities of resident witness even more. We should then
have to devise new plans and methods. The work is not
finished. And the door is not closed.

At about the same time that we transferred operations to
France the administrative organization was modified to take
advantage of the new situation. The former Field Director,
Harold W. Stalley, became Secretary General in 1967 and a new
Field Director, Bernard Collinson, was appointed in his place.

In addition, an International Executive Committee was created to serve at six month intervals between the stated meetings of the International Council. The purpose behind these changes was the desire that the Mission leadership be able to keep in close touch with rapidly changing political and social events in North Africa, in order to make any necessary adjustments promptly. Also, it was intended that the Secretary General would have more time in which to encourage the development of the NAM bases in the homelands; and perhaps extend such bases into new countries.

Two years later another step was contemplated. Many felt that the process of transferring executive leadership from the home council to the field, first begun when Mr. Warren was appointed Field Secretary in 1939 and advanced with the appointment of a Field Director (1952), who was later called the Secretary General should be carried further with the appointment, under the I. C., of a General Director as the chief executive officer of the whole Mission with directive authority over all councils in the homelands as well as on the field. Some were reluctant to go so far so soon, so only a partial step was taken. The Secretary General became International Secretary with slightly increased authority. It was not until 1973 that the whole Mission fully supported the idea of a fully empowered chief executive officer called General Director. This step was finally taken, however, at the I. C. of that year when the Council appointed Abram Wiebe General Director Designate to take office two years later at the 1975 I. C. Meanwhile he worked closely with Mr. Stalley in order to assure a smooth transition.

Once again we see the wisdom of God in His providing just the right leader for us as we planned to pursue aggressively plans for the development of independent national churches in North Africa in the face of tightening political control on the one hand and increasing personal response by North Africans on the other. The times called for a man of deep personal piety, clear foresight regarding the future and disciplined thinking and planning. Such a man is Abram (Abe) Wiebe.

Abe developed habits of personal discipline as he grew up on a farm in a Mennonite community of Western Canada. Raised in a strong Christian family, Abe gave his life to the authority of Jesus Christ at age 19. Graduating from Briercrest Bible Institute in Saskatchewan, he took two more years at Columbia Bible College before going out in 1962 to Morocco for language study. In 1964 he met and married Miss Joyce Morgan who came from Vermont.

After five years in Casablanca the Wiebes were transferred to Oran to head up the team there. A year later he became the Regional Superintendent for Algeria serving as pastor/administrator for the missionaries there. When nominations for General Director Designate were requested, Abe was unanimously put forward by the Field Council as a man who "assembled the facts, reached a firm decision, then led out the team."

Thus we see the growth of NAM from one Home Council in England with the Honorary Secretary located in London in 1883, to four Home Councils (and three Auxiliary Councils, one each in Holland, Germany and France) with the General Director located in Aix-en-Provence, France by 1980. On the other hand, there were very nearly as many missionaries on the field in 1900 as there were as we approached 1980.

At the 1975 International Council Mr. Stalley, the retiring International Secretary, shared some reminiscences and convictions relating to his 24 years of service in NAM leadership. He said that when he became the first really resident field leader of the Mission as Field Director in 1951 God gave him a verse from the book of Isaiah as a promise for the developments of the future, "Behold, I will do a new thing; now it shall spring forth" (Isaiah 43:19). And indeed it was a new thing. An ex-Algiers Mission Band missionary becomes Field leader of the NAM. Reinforcements begin coming from North America. To be sure, NAM lost its legal status in North Africa. But the Mission begins to grow again and the national church to emerge.

Not at all surprisingly I myself took comfort from this same verse when God led me from the academic world of teaching and research in archaeology to assume responsibility for the development of a strong base of interest in NAM in North America. We discovered later that God had given us both the same verse for essentially the same type of work though in

H. GRATTAN GUINNESS—One of the founders of the Mission.

GEORGE PEARSE—Member of the original Committee. He established the first station.

EDWARD F. GLENNY—First Honorary Secretary. He directed the Mission for the first forty years.

LILIAS TROTTER—Founder and early leader of the Algiers Mission Band.

JOHN ANDERSON—Founder of the Southern Morocco Mission.

CUTHBERT NAIRN—First missionary of the Southern Morocco Mission. He was martyred in Marrakech.

HUGHINA TULLOCH—Nurse from Scotland who died of typhus in 1886. The Mission hospital in Tangier was named after her.

HARVEY FARMER—Leader of the Mission in Great Britain. He made his first visit to North America in 1927.

THOMAS WARREN—Missionary to Algerian Kabyles, later Field Superintendent.

WILLIAM REID—Ran a medical clinic in Tripoli, Libya, for many years.

DR. DAVID COOPER—Killed by a fanatical Muslim in Casablanca, 1900.

DR. AND MRS. CHARLES LEACH—Murdered by thieves seven months after their arrival in Sfax, Tunisia, 1896.

EMMA HERDMAN—Developed a unique ministry in Fes supervising Moroccan male colporteurs.

REV. JAMES STEPHENS—Outstanding missionary-minded pastor of Highgate Road Baptist Chruch, London.

EVAN SHORT and FAMILY—Their daughter Helen (later Mrs. Cyril Morriss) age four, is seated front row right.

HAROLD AND VIOLET FIFE—Harold was Chairman of the British Council in 1945. He organized the American (1948) and Canadian (1951) Councils.

HAROLD STALLEY—Missionary of the Algiers Mission Band. Later he was the first Field Director of the NAM.

EDWARD A. STEELE—Member of the original Council in America. He gave major leadership to the development in North America.

REV. AND MRS. ROBERT I. BROWN—Missionaries to Tunisia. Mr. Brown was later Deputy Field Director and finally Chairman of the English Council.

DR. FARNHAM ST. JOHN—Medical Director of the Tulloch Memorial Hospital until it was expropriated in 1974.

BERNARD COLLINSON—Missionary to Algerian Kabyles, later Field Director of NAM.

ABRAM J. WIEBE—Missionary to Morocco and Algeria, later General Director of NAM.

FRANCIS R. STEELE—Member of the American Council 1949-53, and then Home Secretary.

GREGORY M. LIVINGSTON—Director for America of NAM since 1977.

different areas of the Mission's operation. I have enjoyed very much and also benefited greatly from our association together over these years. It seems to me that Mr. Stalley's vision, personal discipline and gracious spirit eminently qualified him to give NAM leadership during these years of transition and growth.

At the same I. C. Mr. Wiebe suggested a definite goal for the appearance of national indigenous churches in North Africa. In his report he asks, "Would it be unrealistic to envisage the establishment of truly indigenous groups within the next few years?" Then he stated his personal convictions, "I believe Morocco should see a minimum goal of two indigenous assemblies by 1985," and later on he said the same about Algeria and Tunisia. In 1976 these goals were expanded to comprise 25 churches during the next ten years in all three countries and double our Mission personnel in order to assist toward this goal.

It was significant, I think, that most of the men who had devotional messages at the beginning of each day's session of the 1975 I. C. were led to take verses from the book of Nehemiah. The final message by Abe Wiebe was built on the verse he believed God had specially given him as the theme for his first term of service, "Le us rise up and build" (Nehemiah 2:18). There was certainly much in the situation that confronted Nehemiah which had parallels in the job before us.

And then there was the question of merger beyond the absorption of the AMB and SMM. There has been considerable talk among mission societies—as well as suggestions made to them by concerned friends—about the wisdom of joining several small groups with common interests for the purpose of economy and efficiency. In fact several missions have actually linked up. But in nearly every case I know of it was a larger mission absorbing a smaller one rather than two separate groups blending together as a new entity. At any rate the idea was broached at the 1969 I. C. and steps were taken to investigate the feasibility of such an action for NAM. At first it was the Middle East General Mission and Africa Inland Mission who were considered as possible partners. But since no clear concensus on the part of the NAM family followed these studies the matter was dropped. It rose again, however, when conversations between leaders in NAM and Sudan Interior Mission revived the consideration of merger. But once again there was not sufficient agreement to consummate merger. There seemed to be some misunderstanding in some quarters regarding the rationale for merger. Some people in the Mission felt that the world-wide economic problems would bring increasing pressures upon Christians in the homelands so that it would be very difficult if not almost impossible for smaller missions to stay alive. In that case merger was tantamount to survival; merge or perish, as it were. Others reacted strongly to this idea concluding that if a smaller mission sought merger on these grounds it would be merge and vanish as far as any distinctive ministry or mandate for the smaller or weaker mission was concerned.

In any case, it was finally decided that in spite of the probable advantage of administrative efficiency at home that merger might provide we should maintain our own identity, tighten up administrative procedures, strengthen promotional activities and trust God to give us the growth in personnel and programs which would advance His work toward the national church in North Africa.

Yet the goal of the General Director still looms ahead of us. To be sure, one of the twenty-five national churches has emerged. In December 1979, the group in the city of Algiers elected elders and became the first truly national church in North Africa for centuries. There are at least six other worshipping groups in North Africa who may well soon take this courageous step also. They need prayer and encouragement. And we need many more highly qualified laborers to strengthen our ranks.

The battle for the Church is not over. But we may well be nearer the "beginning of the end than we are to the end of the beginning."

LINKING UP WITH NORTH AMERICA

Partnership between Britain and North America was a long time growing. Individuals from across the Atlantic were involved in NAM from time to time many years ago. In 1883 Mr. Baldwin from North Carolina was the first man to initiate medical work in Tangier. The following year the Tulloch Memorial Hospital grew from this beginning. Then there were others such as Miss Cowell from Canada. But the first definite effort in involving North America was when Mr. Harvey Farmer (later Doctor when he received a D. D. from Dallas Theological Seminary) set out in 1927 to establish an Auxiliary Council and undertake an extensive deputation ministry in order to acquaint Christians in North America with the needs in North Africa. According to a report in the magazine of July-August 1926, Mr. Farmer's trip was inspired by the fact that "several stations are understaffed and there are open doors everywhere" coupled with the remark that "young lives are offering for service to carry the Gospel abroad, but cannot be sent until the means are at hand to send them."

Incredibly this first trip across the ocean was planned in part, so we are told, because Dr. Farmer's health was in poor shape and it was thought that a change might be helpful. What a generous and optimistic view of the rigors of travel in the "colonies" they must have had in England to entertain such thoughts!

In any case, in September of 1927 the Farmers arrived and fixing a base of operation in Philadelphia started out for about a year on the deputation trail. He returned to North America for a second time at the close of 1930 and, having established a permanent base at the home of Mr. Charles Grant in Philadelphia, continued to serve as Honorary Secretary until his death in 1949. From all reports, and the memory of many friends still living, Dr. Farmer had an unusually effective ministry. He is still widely known as "the man with the beard" who so eloquently showed forth in his life the Spirit of the Lord Jesus he so ardently preached. However, apart from an unknown number of persons who were led to pray for the work, there was little else to show for those years of faithful service except a half dozen recruits, only three of whom were still in NAM by 1948; although two others remained in North Africa as independent missionaries. By the way, it is amusing to note that in the British magazine on the page adjacent to the notice of the

Farmers' first trip to North America there was an article
entitled "First Days in Enemy Territory;" a little startling
until one discovers that the article actually reported the arrival
of a new missionary in North Africa, not the Farmers' visit to
North America. It is unfortunate that no significant base of
interest and support resulted from this unusually fine ministry.
But no effort was made to consolidate the response by establishing an office to collect the names of interested people and
maintain that interest by providing regular notices of current
field information or to follow up the first visits and strengthen
the earlier response. And so it was that when Mr. Harold Fife
arrived in May of 1948 he had to begin all over again. But he
had to begin first in Britain.

Just after the war the Mission passed through what was very
likely its most serious crisis thus far. Missionary giving had
fallen generally in Britain. The government Treasury had
placed severe restrictions on the export of sterling. The Chairman of the Council retired. The Honorary Treasurer died. The
senior doctor at TMH resigned and left with four of the nurses
to set up a private clinic. Things looked pretty grim. But God
had a man for the job.

In late 1946 the Rev. Harold W. Fife joined the British
Council. Mr. Fife was at that time the pastor of St. James Hall,
Worthing. Shortly after that he left for the first of three visits
to the field over a period of eighteen months. There was a great
need for liaison and counselling which he was admirably suited
to fulfill. The following year the pressure of duties related to
NAM grew so great he resigned his pastorate to give himself
full-time to the work of the Mission. He left for North America
in the fall of 1948 and spent three months, not only in
deputation in strategic locations, but also in reviving the
Auxiliary Council established some years earlier in America.
Three years later he organized a new Auxiliary Council in
Canada. His message was short and to the point. In effect he
said, "The war is over. The door to North Africa is open. But we
in Britain lack the resources to move ahead as we should like.
Come over and help us."

It is not clear just what authority he had to do this. It may be
that he had only been charged by the London Council to

encourage the Auxiliary Councils in order to ensure a steadier if not greater flow of support; meaning, of course, money and perhaps recruits for England. On the other hand, he was probably astute enough to judge aright the temper of the "colonists" and realize that the only way to gain maximum support from North America was to grant some real responsibility. Anyway, the two groups were called Councils not just Auxiliaries. But change of name alone means nothing. Aggressive leadership is what produces results.

Once again, as before, God had a man as the instrument chosen to give that kind of leadership and produce an active growing work. That man was Mr. Edward Steele, a business man in Philadelphia. Steele had received great blessing from the Bible studies conducted by the members of the Officers Christian Union in London which he had attended as an American naval officer during World War II. His name was therefore known in Christian circles in London and so Mr. Fife knew of him and invited him to be a member of that new Council.

It is not possible to overestimate the significance of Harold Fife's leadership of NAM at this time. His vision served not only to pull things together in England but also to help set a new course for developments in the future through genuine partnership with Christians in North America. In all of this he had the advice and support of Mr. Harold Stalley, who later became the first Field Director of NAM.

But to return to developments in America; it has never been Ed's nature to join anything just to belong. If he joined, he had to get involved. And that is exactly what he did; completely. In a short time he had gathered around him a small group of men who, though they previously knew almost nothing about missions and absolutely nothing about North Africa, were challenged by his enthusiasm and believed that God intended them to get the evangelical Church in America involved in the Gospel ministry to North Africa. Believe me, it was an intensive learning experience; I was one of that small group. In 1954, at the request of the Canadian group, the two Councils were merged into one North American Council. The Headquarters were located in Philadelphia because Ed was still the major force in those early days.

Following two extensive deputation trips across North America by Robert I. Brown, a British missionary from Tunisia who was invited to help get things under way, it became necessary to appoint a full-time representative for NAM in North America. The flow and pressure of work was too much by then for part-time business men to handle, no matter how dedicated they were.

I was appointed chairman of a committee to find our first Home Secretary. Five months later I found myself in the job. This was another example of God's unusual though unmistakable leading. I had no personal experience as a missionary or in missions for that matter, except for a one year stint as staff member of IVCF and less than four years experience serving on the American Council of NAM. At the time I was Assistant Professor of Assyriology at the University of Pennsylvania. But as far as experience in missions to Muslims, I could only claim a summer's course in Arabic at Princeton University, three seasons living in an Arab village while engaged in archaeological excavations in southern Iraq and a trip home from Iraq which took my wife and me all across North Africa where we visited nearly all the stations and met many of the missionaries. These, together with a willingness to learn, were my credentials.

A year later God added to our growing American office Miss Mary Melville as General Manager. Mary had served for fifteen years with a mission to the Jews in Detroit, Michigan and had engaged in visitation, Bible teaching and some administration. For the next three years she managed a large Bible and Book Shop also in Detroit. So she was well prepared to handle all phases of a new and expanding mission office. We served together for over twenty years as others have come and gone.

Up to 1951 NAM was governed from London by the London Council. But with the creation of two more Home Councils, we were faced administratively with a three-headed monster; an abnormality in any organization. The only solution was to join the three home councils into a supervisory body and create a Field Council for administrative purposes. Easier said than done. However, a Committee was established to consider these matters and attempt a resolution of the problem. This Committee met during the month of January, 1951, in Philadelphia. It consisted of two members of the British Council, the Chairman, H. W. Fife and Harold W. Stalley, formerly a missionary in Algeria with Algiers Mission Band, now a pastor in England; and three members of the American Council, the Chairman, Ed Steele with Paul Hopkins and Francis Steele. Borrowing from the experience of recognized, established missions, the committee soon drafted a Constitution suitable to the needs of our combined work in North Africa. This Consitution included an International Council with representation from the Home Councils and a Field Administration consisting of a Field Director, Deputy Field Director and Field Treasurer. Now the nearest to this structure the Mission had ever approached before was when Mr. Thomas Warren served as Field Superintendent. But he actually lived in France most of the time and exercised more of a pastoral role than an administrative officer. In fact it was clearly stated that he served only as liaison. Effective control and authority remained with the London Council. So the idea of an International Council and Field Administration was indeed a significant departure from earlier days; and it was not immediately seen as an improvement by all members of the Mission.

However, there was a two-fold purpose behind this move. First, of course, overall supervision of the Mission had to be in a body representing all Home Councils. But, equally important, day to day direction of the ministries of the Mission belongs on the Field. So the International Council concerns itself largely with policy and oversight of the Field Administration, whereas operations on the field are the responsibility of Field officers.

But there was still the big question regarding the persons qualified to fill these Field positions. Few senior missionaries on the field had administrative experience and all were occupying strategic though undermanned stations. By the conclusion of the meeting, however and in answer to prayer it was quite clear that the man of God's choice for Field Director was Harold Stalley. So he was nominated for the post and ratified by the British Council. A year later Mr. Stalley set up Field Headquarters in Tangier where he was joined five years later by Clyde Harvey as Field Treasurer. Robert I. Brown, appointed Deputy Field Director, remained in Tunis.

The first meeting of the International Council convened
seventy years after the founding of the Mission. As was entirely
appropriate, Harold Fife was appointed the first Chairman. It
was a rather unusual meeting, but at least it was a start.
The Council met in London and consisted of the whole British
Council, plus Francis Steele of the American Council, who was
on his way out to Iraq for an archaeological expedition. The
chief purpose of that meeting was, I suppose, merely to
recognize the existence of the Council. However, I have one
vivid recollection of the proceedings. I had been instructed by
the American Council to see that allowances for men and
women were equalized. Up to that time men always received
more than women and at that time the allowance rates were 15
pounds for men and 13 pounds for women. After a brief
discussion which included references to the fact that there was
not enough money to pay such amounts—women outnumbered
men on the field eight to one and so forth—it was finally agreed
that the allowance should be 15 pounds for both. This was the
first of many American influences on a British work.

Mr. Fife continued to serve as Chairman for six years until
being replaced by Arch Stewart from Toronto, Canada. Twelve
years later, Rev. Lawrence Luffburrow from America became
Chairman and served four years. During this time he was also
Chairman of the North American Council of which he had been
a member since 1952. His knowledge and able leadership over
this period gave continuity while the Mission was passing
through some difficult times of adaptation to change in North
Africa.

It was certainly the hope that the new outreach of NAM into
North America would soon provide assistance to the be-
beaguered forces in the U. K. And, in fact, it did. But not
necessarily in the way it was expected. By 1953 North America
initiated an adoption program for needy British missionaries.
As interest in North America grew concerning the work in
North Africa, people began to pray and give. Funds came in
faster than recruits. However, at just this time Britain was
passing through another period of financial stringency so it was
proposed that some of the needy missionaries who were dependent on the General Fund be put in touch with some of the

growing numbers of potential supporters in North America. This proved to be a good way not only to build strong personal ties between the ongoing work on the field and the newly developing constituency in North America, but also to share in the financial burden of the work as a whole. In fact, there was precedent for such sharing. Several English missionaries were already receiving prayer and even financial support from America as a result of friendships made during World War II. Many American soldiers who took part in the North African campaign had met British missionaries there who were active in programs for service men. This was especially true in Morocco. In fact, some of these soldiers date their conversions from these contacts. As a result, not only did the missionaries gain partners as supporters but, in a few cases, colleagues, since some of those soldiers actually returned to North Africa later on as missionaries.

As the work of NAM grew in North America some adjustments became necessary. Mr. Edward Steele who had previously been Secretary took over the increasingly demanding responsibilities as Chairman of the American Council. Rev. Eric Fife, brother of Rev. Harold Fife the British Chairman, was invited to leave his church in Winchester, England, to become Deputation Secretary for North America. Also, at the request of the Canadian Council members, the two councils, Canadian and American, merged in 1954 to become the North American Council. After all, the population densities in North America follow two major vertical patterns, one on the east coast and the other on the west coast, not the horizontal pattern of the Canadian-American border. And since the early development of interest in NAM was largely centered in the northeast, it seemed best to consolidate the base of operation where most of the action was. This situation continued for the next twenty-five years until a major expansion of activity in North America led to the reconstitution of the Canadian Council as an independent operation with its own office and David Lundy, formerly a missionary to India with Operation Mobilization, as Director.

Also in 1954 a Field Treasurer was found for the Field Administration. Thus far the Field Director, Harold Stalley, worked out of his modest office in Tangier—one room in Hope

House which was attached to TMH—while his Deputy, Robert Brown, was located in Tunis at the opposite end of the field. Two and a half years after Mr. Stalley set up shop God provided a colleague in the person of Mr. Clyde Harvey from Schenectady, New York. At that time he was working in the finance office of the General Electric Company. Shortly thereafter Clyde and Dottie found themselves in Tangier where he set up the accounts of the mission and continued to manage quite dextrously the increasingly complicated financial affairs of the NAM dealing in nearly a dozen different national currencies among six home offices and four different countries of Mission work.

In 1957 Eric Fife left NAM to become Missionary Secretary for IVCF. He had developed a special interest in student work during his years with NAM and had a fruitful ministry among them. This change was by no means a total loss to the Mission as he carried into IVCF his interest in North Africa. That same year Rev. C. Gordon Beacham joined us as Administrative Secretary. Mr. Beacham brought to us wide experience in all phases of missionary work. He had served for forty years with the SIM, first as a pioneer in Nigeria, then as a field leader in evangelism, literature and radio. It was a clear evidence of gracious, spiritual maturity that a man of his accomplishments was able to put up with the novices in NAM. We benefited tremendously from his practical experience over years of dealing with people and problems in missionary work. He served for eleven years before he retired to live in Florida.

In 1969 we called Rev. William Bell back from his field position as Director of RSB to give administrative leadership to the office in Upper Darby, Pennsylvania. There had been economic pressures and other problems hindering our expected growth. Nevertheless, the decline in income and applications continued in spite of all efforts to turn the situation around. Goals prayerfully set by the Council year by year were not met. So the Council was forced to take steps cutting back expenses at the home end. A large office building was sold and we moved back to smaller rented quarters. Several staff personnel were let go and other economy measures were effected.

This was a grievous disappointment to us since we were

aware of the need for more personnel on the field and more funds to expand such vital ministries as RSB. Perhaps God felt we needed this lesson in order that we might better appreciate our complete dependence on Him.

At any rate, the time soon came when Bill Bell was needed back in France to head up the Missionary Training Center program so we had to accede to the decision of the Field Council and release him for that important post in 1976. Now, what about leadership for the American office? Again, God in His faithfulness provided the man especially qualified to match the challenges of apathetic conventional Christianity and capture some of the enthusiasm of a new breed of Christians in our changing American cultural scene. That man was Rev. Gregory M. Livingston.

Greg had known of NAM seventeen years before, but had decided that Operation Mobilization had more to offer. For twelve years he served as a leader of OM teams in India, Lebanon and Europe as well as heading up work in Canada. But he never lost his dream of personal involvement in a church-planting mission to Muslims. Having withdrawn from OM in 1974, he became pastor of a church in his home town, Aspen, Colorado. Greg met Bill Bell at the 1976 Urbana Convention and told him, "Don't forget, I'm still interested in getting involved with Muslims." Eight months later Greg was installed as Director for North America of the NAM and things began to hum; if not roar.

Recruitment has risen in recent years from about two a year to over twenty and is still growing. The Summer Teams are full each year and are producing very enthusiastic members who spread their excitement among their friends at home. So we praise God and keep on trusting.

DIARY OF TRIP TO NORTH AFRICA, 1957

In 1957 my wife and I travelled across the field from east to west, from Libya to Morocco. She kept a diary of that trip.

Morocco and Tunisia had just gained independence while Algeria was still locked in a painful struggle with France for hers. What we saw—and she recorded—will, I think, give a

vivid picture of conditions at that time. New recruits had been
arriving from North America for several years. And contacts
were beginning to be made with students in North Africa. Other
changes had taken place also; travel was quicker and safer,
technical services had improved, medical and educational facilities were more numerous and increasing all the time. But the
grip of Islam was just as strong as ever on countries and people.

Tripoli   March 4/5
Arrived Tripoli at 11:30 P.M. Beautiful, clear starlit skies. Met
by Dr. Pat McCarthy, still possessed of his jovial sense of
humor. Also by Khalifa, a friend who helped us through
customs, and one for whom prayer is needed. He has made a
profession of Christ very recently—is it real?

Tripoli   March 5
Pat showed us through the adjoining house, formerly used as a
nurse's residence. We could also see over the wall into the
"cottage," now condemned and being inhabited by a squatter.
The plan is to eject him, raze the ruins, and use it for a men's
clinic. At present, the nurse's home is *stacked* with materials
given to Pat by friends at Wheelus Field, the USAF base
nearby, including beds enough for the proposed hospital, if and
when.

Tripoli: Clinic Day   March 6
233 patients treated. Every possible sort of complaint. Saw
many, many under-nourished babies (one nearly dead with
pneumonia), all sorts of eye disease. What a pathetic picture of
the results of ignorance and superstitution. Many children with
cigarette burns on their stomachs, parents and relatives thinking to "burn" out their illness. Poor creatures—"Unto you is
born a Savior." Oh, that they might know Him! The boys' class
in the afternoon got a bit noisy and out of hand. Doubtless
because we were there and they wanted to show off. Boys will
be boys, everywhere!

Tripoli   March 7
Off early in Major Wood's Chevy for a day at Leptis Magna, 70
miles east of Tripoli on the Mediterranean Sea. What a place!
The ruins are in quite good preservation. Everywhere beautiful

marble columns and ornate capitals. The baths were being excavated. Lavish affairs with a half dozen rooms heated to various temperatures, and all around statues to help one's aesthetic enjoyment. The theater was another very interesting place, with its great amphitheater facing toward the sea, stage down below. Again very full of statues on each aisle and generously scattered about. One could almost picture the wealthy Romans riding up in their carriages to attend a performance of some Greek play. Then back to the area of the markets, the Law Courts, etc. A huge area of the Law Courts had been adapted for use as a Christian church and one can still plainly see the baptistry and the pulpit standing out in the middle of the huge court. Here were the most beautiful sculptured marble pillars. The port area and the old harbor were also fascinating. We could climb up atop of what might have been a watchtower or lighthouse and see the whole city spread out to the south. The old anchorage spots were spaced along the quay, and it must have provided a busy scene as the ships came, loaded and unloaded, and sailed out to the sea again.

Finally, weary and sunburned we returned to the car and thence over the desert to Tripoli. The poor land is dotted with flocks, some scattered Bedouin tents, and poor shacks made of grass mats and tin cans. Everywhere, poverty, ignorance and disease. What a needy place! But Jesus loves them all! May we love as He did!

Tripoli   March 8
Visited the girls' class in the afternoon. Vivian and Margaret taught by rote. Vivian gave an object lesson about a kerosene lamp. Girls were very responsive and intelligent. Afterward they gathered on benches in the courtyard for embroidery and knitting instructions.

Then Vivian and I went to the El Hadi's house for tea. He is the silk weaver whose daughter Badriya helps in the clinic. His wife, Zohra, 33, was seated on a mattress in a narrow room hung with pink silk drapes. The other children, Aisha, a very fat 3 year old, and two boys aged 7 and 10, gathered around politely. We "talked," that is, Vivian, translated. El Hadi is very proud of his family and shows an uncommon love for them all. Badriya read to us from her school books and showed us her pictures. We went through the ritual of three cups of tea, poured back and forth to produce a lot of foam and only a small amount of liquid. After about an hour a bag of unshelled peanuts was brought and as we talked, El Hadi and the children shelled them, roasted them over the pot of charcoal and the last cup of tea was served full of peanuts.

Zohra proudly dressed me in all her finest clothes. She got discouraged trying to get my short hair to look like hers—a long thin pigtail tied with string, and two thin strands outside the kerchief drawn down one side of her face, a la Garbo. But she finally managed to tie a purple kerchief around my head. When later, Zohra's aunt came in, she was delighted and pleased that I was in their costume. El Hadi got the bright idea of having me go for treatment to Dr. McCarthy in disguise. So an outer haik (cloak) was wrapped about me and through a small triangular peep hole, I followed her through the street around to the mission house. It was all a very great joke when I unveiled in the examination room.

Tripoli   March 10
We drove off after breakfast to "Little America," that is, Wheelus Field. Fran taught the adult Bible class, joined by the junior adult Bible class, on John 8. Very well received and taught. Church followed where he also had a brief opportunity to say a word for the Mission.

After that we had dinner at the Woods' home, an army Major. Harold Stalley was also with us. After a quiet afternoon, we came over en mass to the Mission for a private evening fellowship, including a celebration of the Lord's Supper.

Tripoli   Sunday, P.M.
We all met together at the Mission for a discussion of "station business." Especially the future of medical work in Tripoli. It appears to be the will of God to plan an immediate extension of the clinic on the property adjoining the present mission house. If permission is granted for the hospital, however, we will begin work on that in preference to clinic expansion. In other words, a flexible operation including both projects in one.

Tripoli   Tuesday, March 12
Packed early and hasted about some urgent errands. Patsy had
invited Khalifa's family in for a couscous dinner, which they
had brought. We sat around on cushions, shoeless, and all ate
out of the common bowl. Harold Stalley led in a Bible reading
from Luke and prayed at the close. All three young men seemed
interested in the Scriptures, especially Khalifa. After the usual
good-byes, we took off for Tunis.

It was quite an interesting flight, affording a good view of
Tripoli, the sandy orchard groves and out to sea. We stayed
rather close along the shore, and the whole way along were
impressed by the barren land. A very interesting coast line with
many long bars, spits, etc. Flew across the Isle of Djerba, part
of Tunisia, about 14 miles in length and with approximately
7,000 inhabitants. Landing at the west end of the island, we saw
the local inhabitants in the characteristic bernous, and women
with heavy silver anklets. Also *on parle francais ici.*

Another stop at Sfax, and then on to Tunis where we landed
about 6 P.M. Mr. Stanley Miles and Warren Gaston met us and
we drove directly to Warren's home, a very modern apartment
of five rooms, furnished in modern furniture. Quite a contrast to
mission properties in Tripoli or almost anywhere else. We sense
discouragement resulting from recent trials, and it is further
proof that contentment in Christ is not at all related to physical
surroundings.

Tunis   Wednesday, March 13
Our first meeting was at 10 A.M. Present: Miles, Ada Clack
and Mabel Jones, Rickards, Gastons, Steeles, Stalley and Alma
Strautins. Fran led us in a time of devotions and we had prayer
for needs on the field. According to custom here, the whole gang
ate together in a restaurant downtown. Another time of fellowship and prayer at 3 P.M. followed by tea. In the evening we all
came together again for further fellowship. II Corinthians 10.
"Ye are all one Bread," and a feast together around the Lord's
table.

Tunis   Thursday, March 14
After breakfast, the whole gang met for their annual business
meeting. The singing on this station is very good and they all

seem to enjoy it. Midge Gaston spread the table for us and the Sousse gals, Ada Clack and Mabel Jones. We left for Sousse soon after. The trip down was largely on straight flat ground, through mountains on the west and sea to the east. We passed very fertile fields, olive groves, and citrus orchards. Also many little troglodyte-sort of dwellings, and Bedouin camps, tattered tents, sleepy little villages, etc. Everywhere is evidence of European evacuation and Arabic taking over.

Sousse   Friday, March 15
After breakfast, we set off for a tour of the Sousse Museum and the old catacombs. We had fun photographing quite a few objects and Dr. Raucher, the curateur, seemed to enjoy the visit of a fellow archaeologist. Drove a bit around this fascinating place and got back in time for tea. Then the girls took us around through the native section on foot. This whole city is busy preparing for the independence celebration; taking down all their French signs and replacing with Arabic.

Tunis   Saturday, March 16
Fran drove us back to Tunis. The girls, Ada and Mabel, with their "flus" (money) for their new Citroen. The Miles entertained us at a lovely French meal. Their attractive, antique apartment really intrigued us. It is part of one of the palaces of the Turkish rulers long ago. After dinner they drove us out to Carthage, with a stop-off at the American Cemetery. The place has really changed since our visit seven years ago. White marble crosses, a lovely reception room and a chapel, all furnished in beautiful elegance. Also, the Carthage remains have been all landscaped with beautiful flowers, and many more things unearthed.

Tunis   Sunday, March 17
We enjoyed the Bethesda morning worship conducted in French. Don Rickards translated a brief meditation from Fran and a Brethren-style fellowship followed, concluded by the Lord's Supper. Sunday afternoon we had a lovely tea at the Miles' home and took quite a few pictures. It was really a family time. And then in the evening, the Rickards, Gastons, and

ourselves met for a small worship service. Margaret looking quite well as usual. However, toward midnight she called for the doctor, and when we awoke in the morning, we had the good word that her wee daughter, Linda, had arrived about 4:30 A.M. Poor Midge had been up nearly all night in attendance, but somehow managed to keep going.

Tunis   Monday, March 18
As soon as we were dressed, we all trouped up to see Margaret and the baby—quite the youngest I had ever seen. She lay as a tiny bundle alongside her mother, happy and relaxed. Then Mrs. Miles, Alma Strautins and I went off to visit in the native homes. The first house (in the village of Saida) was down an indescribably dirty street, with all the refuse lying in a gutter that really stank. Twisting and turning, we found our way to Aziza's little dwelling. The gate opened into a tiny courtyard in which lay a fierce dog. No uninvited guest could safely enter there! Inside the main room we saw Aziza and her friend, a woman pregnant and therefore firmly seated on a straw mat. Behind her, a cot with several blankets in a heap, one small table and a bed at the other end. As we sat on the bed and talked, a white bundle behind the one woman moved and from within came some crying sounds. A little three year old girl, sick, possibly with pneumonia and also measles. The mother feared she might lose her eyesight, a common result there. (Aziza has born 13 children, but only three have survived. She has worked nine years for Mrs. Miles and at one time made a profession of faith in Christ.) Later Mrs. Miles gave a lap-board message of the lost lamb. The seated friend listening was ever so attentive, but at the end she said that Muhammed would take care of her sins, she didn't need Jesus. How sad! How blind! After a bit more conversation we departed, walking up the hill out of the mud flat on which the village is built. We passed several old, bent women, burdened under gas tins filled with water which they must carry from the top of the hill, which is the edge of Tunis City. If I had the job, my back would be broken I fear, and I am sure I would not bother nearly so much about cleanliness! They don't! We walked to Mebrouka's house, a much better place, but still miserable by any of our standards.

She is a Christian girl, but married to a strict Muslim. Though only 30, she was about to have her sixth child. Her mother, also, is a Christian. Her children came in eagerly to hear the Gospel story, told by Alma this time. We really had a sweet visit there. But one cannot but pity the poor girl who has no spiritual companions and who lives under such poverty and need.

As we taxied back to the city, the whole place manifested great excitement because Vice-President Richard Nixon had just arrived to celebrate with them the first anniversary of their independence. There was really a great spirit of hope and expectancy for a great Tunisia. May we take advantage of their "pro-West" leanings to preach to them the unsearchable riches of Christ. In the evening we again had prayer fellowship—a short one since we were all dreadfully weary, and then said our farewells all around.

Algiers   Tuesday, March 19
Off at 7:15 A.M. by Air Tunis for Algiers. It was a most beautiful trip across sharp mountains dipping to the blue, blue sea, and fresh green farmlands. Clarence Adams met us in the modern new airport and we drove through a heavily industrial area into the heart of Algiers. One could not see any difference between this and a modern European city. High up a hill south of the center of town is the villa now inhabited by the Browns above and the Adams below. For the gathering, the Ewings and the Collinsons had come. Mr. Coffee was visiting from England. Kay Castle and Ruth Stewart were also there. So we were crowded around two long tables for our first meal in Algiers. After the evening worship time, a communion service and also the formal reception of Ruth and Kay into the full status of "missionary." It was really a precious time for us all.

Algiers   Wednesday, March 20
Collinsons and ourselves breakfasted with the Adams, and morning prayer followed at 8:30 A.M. Fran spoke on "Missionary Qualifications." Immediately after, I packed up for our two-day stay in Cherchell and we "flew" off in Bob Brown's car, stopping for lunch along the way. The country side is very beautiful, and the sea, that unbelievable blue. Quite hilly, and

high mountains along the southern horizon. After arrival and a
beautiful tea with the Barnetts, Mary Lou took me to call on an
Arab family. In two very tiny rooms, 10 people exist, somehow.
After talking with them awhile, a bent old woman appeared,
groaning and moaning from pain. She, dear soul, is a true saint,
who raised Malika, one of the student nurses in Tangier. Now
she lives an indescribably hard life in a tiny closet of a room,
stretched out on the floor on a mat. Won't heaven be wonderful
release for her? Also she has completely lost her sight. Her son,
in whose home we visited, has these eight children and they are
growing up with the benefit of hearing the Gospel, at least.
Mary Lou left a tin of milk and a large piece of cheese for them.
The little seven month old son has been quite ill and they all
need food. After leaving, we walked a bit through the town,
passing the site of the old carpet school once operated by the
mission. It is the effect of this work that still gives the present
missionaries their chief opportunities. After supper we again
went up for "coffee" hour. And then to bed, but *not* to sleep.
Our window faced upon one of the main streets and throughout
the night there were companies of soldiers marching up and
down and armored trucks roaring by. Algeria is still engaged in
her war for independence. A long siren at 5 A.M. put the whole
town under curfew, and there must have been trouble through
the night. Whatever it is we don't know.

Cherchell   Thursday, March 21
The curfew lasted until 10:30 this morning and we have
employed the last hour in a prayer meeting. When at last we
were allowed out, we wandered leisurely through the town,
along the sea wall, where we saw the little fishing boats in the
harbor and the fishermen's huts along the bank. We went
through the park, a small square filled with broken Roman
columns and some huge old trees, and at length into the market
where we bought a few provisions.

It was rather startling to see a shaven calf's head for sale at
the meat stand. After dinner, the girls arrived for their class.
Zohra had the lesson, reviewing their memory work which
included lengthy passages, and many, many verses. Their
singing was lusty and enthusiastic, and then Zohra told them

the story of the two men who went to pray in the Temple. We gave them greetings from the class in the States, which they really enjoyed, and took quite a few pictures. After tea we went visiting with Zohra into homes that had once been mission properties in the old days of the "Cherchell Carpet School." The homes we visited were neat and clean and very nicely furnished. The modern middle class Arab lives quite nicely. Here again we took quite a few pictures. The next day we drove to Algiers.

Algiers   Saturday, March 23
After breakfast Bob Brown took us downtown in Algiers and we tramped about on several errands. In the afternoon there was a gathering of three fellows at Ruth's apartment. We were most impressed with Aziz, a Kabyle boy of very good education, who appeared in every way like a French or European student. We had a good time chatting together and we pray that God will bless His word to those hearts. We ate at the student restaurant and then all returned to the Browns.

Algiers   Sunday, March 24
This afternoon meeting rather overwhelmed us all with about 50 or 60 in attendance. We recruited every chair imaginable and some quite unimaginable and the salon was completely filled. Fran gave a good word on the "Water of Life," Isaiah 55 and there seemed to be quite genuine interest. The group was a great hodgepodge of missionaries, Europeans and Arabs. We were all very thankful for what the Lord has done in bringing them all together. After supper we had a quiet study of II Corinthians 10 and it proved most helpful to us all.

Djemma Sahridj   Monday, March 25
We got off to a very early start for our drive with Bob Brown to Tizi Ouzou. In Tizi we met Bernard Collinson who took us to visit M. Roland, a French missionary and then M. Abouadaou, an old retired Kabyle Methodist preacher converted by NAM missionaries years ago at Djemma Sahridj. We had brief but genial fellowship in each place. We helped Bernard shop before returning to Djemma. One could not help but be very impressed with the huge numbers of armed soldiers literally flooding the town. We got to Djemma in time for a late dinner and a stroll around the mission property. Then Bernard took us through the

village to visit a sick man. It was truly fascinating to climb down the hard packed path between the walls of stone houses with red-tile roofs and catch sight of the bright-colored skirts and equally bright children's faces around every bend. The home we visited was very interesting, consisting of one room with a stone floor, walls of stone covered with mud, wooden beams, a small hole in the floor for a charcoal fire, and several clotheslines strung up to hold the sleeping mats. After a short stay, we returned by the main road in time for tea, celebrating Kay Castle's birthday of yesterday by sharing a fruit cake sent on from England.

Djemma Sahridj   Tuesday, March 26
We had a very good Bible study just after lunch, in Ephesians 1, with Fran leading. Then, Kay took me along to the home of her Kabyle teacher. We enjoyed the visit in a simple home, but much above the standard of the place the day before. After a bit, Joyce Collinson came along and we went on to visit in Ali's home, again a step up. Very fine furniture, even a separate room for a kitchen, proudly boasting a gas stove. We began to discuss cameras and found that Ali is quite a camera fan. He showed me his dark room which seemed quite well equipped. We drank some fine tea and at last took leave. Then we visited with Tatum, Bel Kassem's daughter, and his widow. Here again was a very nice home, and after a discussion of knitting patterns and sizes, etc., Joyce read a passage from the Scriptures. One could not feel any great warmth here, though Tatum professes to be a Christian. She only seems to tolerate the exercise, but initiates nothing herself. What a pity that so many in Djemma feel they can have a foot in both worlds, Christian and Islam. How we must pray for a *vital* work there.

Djemma Sahridj   Thursday, March 28
Left Djemma after breakfast and enjoyed a beautiful ride back to Algiers.

Algiers   Friday, March 29
This morning we took a fascinating tour around Algiers city. Started in the old area near the sea, and actually walked inside an old mosque and observed the "faithful" performing their

ablutions before prayer time. We wandered a bit in the Casbah
and from the ramparts we got a good view of the old city. We
were surprised to see some veiled Arab women taking candles
into the Roman Catholic Cathedral. What hopelessness and
ignorance! "And Jesus wept over Jerusalem."

Algiers   Saturday, March 30
Left Algiers by air this afternoon with a large crowd to say
farewell. Finally arrived Chez Hollinshead in Casablanca by
8:00 P.M.

Casablanca   Monday, April 1
The southern Morocco gang came together for the monthly
prayer day. Wilsons, Dew, and Coffee, Smetanas and Joyce all
came from Rabat, and we were seven in Casa. The day was well
spent in prayer.

Casablanca   Tuesday, April 2
Visited school at Rue Mannery. Grace Sharp and Marguerite
Hauenstein keep a five day school for about 80 girls. They teach
the "3 R's" as well as Bible. This is the only education available
to girls in Casablanca. We were given full opportunity for
photographs of all the work. We were really drawn to those
workers who under threatenings by the police manifested a
calm, brave trust in the Lord. We had an especially precious
time in the late afternoon with five brave Christian girls, two of
whom were baptised.

Rabat   Thursday, April 4
Visited Miss Dew's boys' class. Enjoyed her flannelgraph
presentation of Cain and Abel. Was quite impressed at the
great difficulties under which she labors, converting her garage
into a classroom, standing against the persistent noise outside
while teaching and so forth. Boys seemed very interested. Tom
took us through the old city, through the shopping area, where
we noticed a shop called "Nouveau Chicago"; a second-hand
clothing store. Toward the end of one street, the leather
merchants were crowded so with their packs of skins that we
could barely get through. We wandered through the Oudaia
fortress climbing up on the top of the old wall from which we

could gain a wonderful view of the city. Found it very impressive with its thick wall and the lighthouse out against the Atlantic. Had a nice visit after dinner with John Barcus from GMU. Fern drove us out to Tour Hassan, another vantage point from which the sea stretches on the one hand, the city hugging up against it, and the rolling plains into the distance. We counted 28 sloping ramps (seven stories) as we descended inside the tower to the ground level. Drove by the Sultan's palace, where we saw some guards in drill, past the fancy high class homes at the edge of town and at last back home.

Rabat   Friday, April 5
Visited the mixed class in Miss Dew's front room. Two older boys do embroidery along with the younger girls. They recited their verses for us, and then Irene gave the flood story in flannelgraph. Even I understood some of the Arabic! We were served couscous dinner in real native style, with the hand washing ceremony first, and everything very proper. At 2 P.M. Fern called for us and we visited the Old Chellah Mosque outside Rabat. It was quite crowded, but we enjoyed wandering through the gardens growing amid the old ruins there. The children really seemed to love the outing.

Fes   Saturday, April 6
Tom drove us and Martha Smetana up to Fes. We stopped in Khemisset, where we met the GMU gang and dined with the Clem Paines. Were shown the print shop, then a ride out to the farm where native and missionary conferences are held, and also a school conducted for missionary children of GMU. It was 3:00 P.M. before we resumed our journey. The bare mountainous country was interesting, but sandy plain stretches in between reminded us of desert lands in Iraq and elsewhere. Certainly this country has not the beauty of Algeria, or the development of Tunisia, but it is still hardly as backward as Libya. Fes, itself, is a curious place, where streets wind around between high blank walls, and all life is lived on the interior.

Fes   Monday, April 8
Visited the women's dispensary. Photographed them all sitting around the courtyard waiting for treatment after Grace Lincoln

preached to them. Then Kinza took us through the medina, a
long tour through narrow streets lined with shops of every
description, brass making, dying, leather-workers, etc. In the
afternoon, we strolled through the new town and then were
driven to the Tour de Fes, a long road winding around through
the hills surrounding the city. "Very like Jerusalem," they say,
with its olive groves, sandy hillsides latticed with goat trails,
much water, etc. After supper, Ben Ali, a Christian nursing
student, came and we enjoyed some fine fellowship in song
together.

Fes   Tuesday, April 9
Grace took us over to the potter's shop where we watched the
fascinating process whereby one rough lump of clay is turned
into several different kinds of vessels by the skill of the potter's
hands, which are then decorated and fired for durability. Left
by train at noon for Alcazar, where we at last arrived about 7:00
P.M. Saw a most remarkable rainbow, a complete double arc
across the whole sky above a quite level stretch of plain. God's
promise is sure, and we stand upon it for this desolate land.
Passed many, many mud hut villages, miserable in the gray of
the drizzling rain. Saw a sheep struggling in a river into which
it slipped while the shepherd was sleeping under his wet cloak.
Truly a sheep without a shepherd.

Alcazar   Wednesday, April 10
Visited Miss Chipperfield's embroidery school where about 20
girls work from 8:00 A.M.—2:00 P.M. on their handwork.
Enjoyed taking their pictures. Harold Stalley gave them a little
word and they sang for us. About 4:00 P.M. we took a stroll
through Alcazar, very depressed by the weaving "factories,"
airless lofts, not high enough for standing, where small children
deftly worked at the looms, or tied knots in the carpets,
crowded together in their dim workrooms all day long, the
auction in the square, the spice sellers with their wares all
spread out in a cloth under some trees. The difference in the
general standard of living here as against the French zone is
very evident. Passed a Koranic school and listened for several
minutes to the almost hypnotic chanting. Enjoyed a brief Bible
study and prayer time.

Tetuan   Saturday, April 13
Peggy and Joe came for me after breakfast and we drove south
of the city up into a mountain road as far as we could safely go.
Then by foot we travelled another couple of miles, wondering at
the mountain beauty. Nestled inside the valley were many little
villages, and the flat land of the valley was all neatly set off into
little wheat fields. The rock hillsides were turned into grape and
fig orchards by dint of much labor. We talked briefly with one
man, a most pleasant fellow who was happy to be photographed, very good looking also. Found ourselves very tired by
the time we regained the car, but felt quite glad for the exercise
and for so much beauty. Saturday night there was an entertain-
ment for about a dozen of Miss Low's English students, a very
interesting group of young men. Before that, we had dined at
one of their homes, Mustapha, a quite wealthy boy, whose home
was very beautiful. The meal was the Ramadan "breakfast,"
starting with a bowl of very peppery soup, a special treat for
this occasion.

Tetuan   Sunday, April 14
We six gathered for a private communion service at the mission
house, which was a real blessing. Sunday evening we visited the
Spanish church, a very lively gathering of true believers. The
friendliest group and healthiest witness we've seen in North
Africa. God is really blessing there. Sunday evening Ashoosha
and her sister Fatima, came over for a visit. Two beautiful girls,
one whose heart really belongs to Christ. We sang together half
in Arabic, and half in English. Then we watched a film strip of
Pilgrim's Progress, again amazed at the wonderful truths there.
Tetuan   Monday, April 15
Dispensary day at Tetuan. Afterwards, Peggy and I went to
Ashoosha's home where we found her beautifully dressed in a
white satin gown waiting for us. She really is a dear and we had
a very sweet time with her and Fatima, her sister still unsaved.
Spent a quiet afternoon and enjoyed a Bible study on Matthew
16 together with Effie and Elsie.

Tetuan   Tuesday, April 16
Visited Tetuan school of fine arts where all the native crafts are
taught and very exquisitely wrought. Had our "picnic" in the

kitchen and after a brief nap, set off for Tangier where we arrived about 5:00 P.M. Mr. Coffee led the evening meditation. Talked with Selma in our room and then visited at Dar en Nour, seeing the Stalleys, Campbells, and Harveys again. How good it is to meet all these folk after all the time apart. Our prayer is increased. May we all be truly blessed of God this coming week! May every heart be freshened and revived, that each one of these splendid people may be useful unto Him and mutually help each other. Our God is able even for this!

Tangier   Thursday, April 18
Had couscous dinner at Dar Scott with the student nurses, Miss Henman and Miss Anderson. We were shown through Radio Station WTAN by Mr. Freed on The Mountain. A very beautiful place and a ministry that God is richly blessing. In the evening, Fran preached on "The Image of the Invisible," and it was a blessed word. Coffee at the Harveys' closed the day.

Tangier   Easter Sunday, April 21
A sunrise service was held on the mountain at which Fran spoke. I, afterwards, heard the tape over the radio at 10:30 A.M. Our Easter 11:00 A.M. service was very blessed, being followed by a communion service. It was partly in English, and partly in Arabic. Some of the Moors were frightened by the sound of stones being thrown onto the roof of the chapel and left before the serving of communion. But others stayed and I am sure were blessed by the presence of the Lord. Of course, this meant "breaking the fast" publicly. In the evening the Dar Scott girls (North Africans) with a few other nurses provided a chorus for the Easter service. Pictures of the death, burial, and resurrection were projected and Tabeeb (Doctor) St. John read Scripture passages in both Arabic and English. The singing was in both languages also, with one number in French as well. It was a truly lovely service and one felt that God was glorified in it all. A blessed Easter Day which lifted all our hearts to praise our risen Lord.

BROADENING THE BASE IN EUROPE

From its inception the North Africa Mission has been a truly international mission. Its present personnel includes nationals from 18 different countries. Although the Mission was directed and funded from England, the first two missionaries were foreigners; one Swiss, the other Syrian. The main reason for this is that two of the three founders, Mr. Pearse and Mr. Guinness travelled often to France and had many French contacts.

There have been many Swiss missionaries since then also. Many Swiss are French speaking Protestants. And the Swiss Missionary Council focusses the missionary interest of evangelical Swiss Christians on world needs and assists Swiss volunteers to find places of service in missionary societies providing support for them as well. In fairly recent years there have been many Swiss and Scandinavian nurses in NAM since Dr. Farnham St. John of TMH frequently vacationed in Europe and had many friends there.

But now the time has come when the Mission is setting up bases in Europe for the express purpose of providing current information for prayer to God's people there and also to present the needs on the field to qualified Christian workers so that those whom God is appointing may join the church-planting teams in North Africa.

The first country to get linked up in this way was Holland. Mr. Hans v. d. Steen representing Trans World Radio met Warren Gaston representing NAM's RSB at a conference for Christian radio broadcasters. Mr. v. d. Steen had heard of the work in North Africa through friends in Trans World Radio and was interested to find out how things were going. Since many Dutch Christians are keenly interested in missionary radio, they soon began supporting the work of RSB and that led to the establishing of an Auxiliary Council in Holland to promote the interests of NAM. They are continuing their support and are beginning to send out missionaries.

The development of NAM interest in Germany stems from an invitation to attend the first missionary conference of the German Student Mission in Deutschland, the German branch

of the Inter Varsity Christian Fellowship (or Inter Varsity
Fellowship of Christian Unions, as it is called in Britain). It
was my privilege to attend this conference in Frankfurt-am-
Main in 1965. I met several keen Christian leaders who, though
at the time not acquainted with NAM, were very much
interested in the Muslim world. I was invited back to Germany
in early 1967 for an extensive deputation tour which eventually
led to the establishing of a Council in the neighborhood of
Essen with several outstanding Christian leaders such as Rev.
Ulrich Parzany, Mr. Hans Steinacher and Mr. Herbert Rein-
hard as members. In 1979 a full-time representative was
appointed to serve the German Council, Mr. Bernard Kreuzer,
former professor of German at Calvin College, Grand Rapids,
Michigan; another example of international cooperation.

At long last an office is being set up in France. For several
years there has been a French organization called Association
Service et Temoinage (ASET) to serve as a cover for such
operations as the Missionary Training Center, General Headquarters and other missionary outreach among Muslims in
France. And many individual French people have had a deep
interest in our work in North Africa. In fact, several serve with
RSB. But the idea to set up an office and staff directly to
represent NAM seeking support and recruits was slow in
appearing. Now, however, Mission Evangelique parmi les Nord-
Africains (MENA) will set about building a contituency in
France. It is a separate organization distinct from ASET. The
membership of the founding committee has been established
and MENA hopes soon to be sending out and supporting
missionaries under NAM.

Whenever any one of these groups reaches the point of
supporting fully ten or more missionaries in NAM the Auxiliary Council will become a full council and a voting member in
the International Council.

RADIO SCHOOL OF THE BIBLE

The Radio School of the Bible developed initially as a
response to the growing need for a more systematic scheme of
Bible study for the increasing numbers of inquirers and con-

verts in North Africa. For some time there were several local programs of correspondence courses being conducted by the personnel of different missions in their own areas. After independence political pressures forced NAM to combine their programs and relocate this ministry in the south of France. In time other departments such as radio and Theological Education by Extension (TEE) were added to provide for further specialized ministries. But the basic thrust for all was a desire to generate a response to the Gospel and then to provide a series of graduated lessons in Bible which would meet the needs of individual inquirers, leading them to saving faith in Christ and competence in the principles of church growth and management.

In early days the focus of ministry in North Africa was the two-fold program of personal witness and literature distribution. But this kind of work is more fluid than substantial. It tends to ebb and flow with the travels of the missionaries and the conditions of the times. Certainly many thousands of people are touched in this fashion and some become real Christians. But it rarely produces a solid, permanent witnessing group in any one place founded on mature and capable national Christian leaders.

Almost from the start missionaries have conducted classes of various kinds for women and children which combined with Bible study such skills as knitting, sewing, reading and writing. Later there were also Bible classes for men. And these ministries were productive up to a point. Yet nothing seemed calculated to lay a foundation for a national church which was the declared goal of the Mission. What was lacking, apparently, was a carefully designed plan to achieve that end.

Begin with the question: What will it take to produce a truly independent national church of converted Muslims? The obvious answer is a cadre of spiritually mature Christians given special training in theology and basic principles of church government. In order to achieve this goal it will be necessary to identify among the converts those with gifts of leadership and institute a training program to help develop those gifts. But, of course, things did not develop so simply. Individual needs were recognized and met as well as possible. Then more advanced

lessons were added as they appeared necessary. It was soon
recognised, however, that there were far more people desiring
and needing the opportunity for Bible study than could be
reached by the few scattered missionaries. Moreover, these
people were also too widely scattered for the missionaries to
reach them and unable themselves to go where the missionaries
lived. Therefore it seemed obvious that the scheme of sending
prepared lessons out by mail was the way to solve the problem;
hence Bible correspondence courses.

The first such effort in North Africa began in Morocco. Here
Robert Schneider of GMU shared his dream with colleagues in
other missions and a cooperative effort distributing thousands
of application forms through the literature ministry at the
Casablanca International Fair got the work fairly launched. A
few years later NAM missionaries began a similar work in
Tunis.

The work in Tunis centered in the bookstore already in
operation. Response was relatively slow at first since, apart
from one or two opportunities to reach large crowds at the
International Fairs, the problem of making the availability of
the courses known was an acute one. A year later, however, a
team of young people with Operation Mobilization arrived and
agreed to distribute our application forms with their own
literature as they travelled throughout Tunisia. The response to
this effort was so great that two of the OM girls remained
behind when the rest of the team left in order to help process the
applications. As time went on students began to gather at the
Center in Tunis for special studies. And there was a Sunday
afternoon preaching meeting addressed by a Tunisian Christian. Admission to it was by invitation only.

After a time rumblings of displeasure were heard, from
Tunisian officials, then protest and warnings. The missionaries
replied that as far as they could see their activities were
protected by the law. But, finally one day in May of 1963, there
came a written order from the police to cease their activity and
the next day the shop was padlocked. The Minister of the
Interior and the Minister of (religious) Education each had
found some of our materials in the possession of their children.

By this time NAM missionaries had started correspondence course ministries in Casablanca and Algiers. These, too, were based on bookstores as centers of operation and were growing slowly. When word arrived that the work in Tunisia had been shut down by the police it was suggested that if the files and materials could be recovered it might be wise to transfer operations to Algiers. However, it took several weeks of negotiating before the records were finally released. By that time the same ominous warnings were being heard in Algiers also.

Now, some time before all this the Field Council, at the direction of the International Council, had begun to study plans for the possible forced evacuation of missionary personnel. They had decided to establish a center in the south of France for this purpose. So when the question as to relocating the Correspondence Course ministries arose, it seemed good strategy to combine the efforts of the three centers in Morocco, Algeria and Tunisia and establish a single base in France. Marseilles, second city of France and a major transportation center in the Mediterranean basin, recommended itself. So Warren Gaston, who had been directing the work in Tunis, moved to France and began to search for suitable quarters.

It appears that there were attacks on this ministry from other than simply human government sources. While engaged in negotiations with the authorities in Tunis, Warren Gaston came down with hepatitis. As pressures grew in Algiers, Irving Hoffman, a partner in the work, developed a brain tumor and had to be flown home for emergency surgery. In Casablanca, Bert Hollinshead, heading the work there, had a heart attack and was invalided home to England. But since this move forward was in God's plan and informed Christians prayed, most of these leaders recovered and were quickly returned to the field and the work kept on.

After some searching Warren Gaston finally located a place in Marseilles which could serve as the new center for the combined ministry. So the staff with all their records and equipment moved into Les Grottes in a high region of Marseilles called Mont Olivet. However, this proved to be only a temporary move since there was no room for expansion and the rent kept going up. That meant start the search all over again. Not long afterwards another property of quite a different kind seemed available. It was an old convent in a nearby town called Aubagne. Although the price seemed reasonable it was a large sum for NAM. We had not spent $40,000 for property for many years in the history of the Mission. Yet the ministry of Bible Correspondence Courses was a strategic and growing arm of the work in a changing world. And God marvelously answered prayer so that the down payment (60 percent of the purchase price) came in quickly.

Then the blow fell. The municipality of Aubagne took over the property and consequently it was no longer available. However, the reaction of the NAM leaders was immediate and positive; this simply means God has something better for us. After five months of praying and searching "the better thing" was found; a cheese factory with living quarters on the second floor, thirteen years old, well-built and situated on a half acre of ground. The price: $115,000! Much better, yes; but also much more expensive. For a Mission that was just making its operating expenses year by year with virtually no excess capital funds at hand that was indeed a sizable goal for us. But if God has planned and led surely He is able. So the whole Mission went to prayer. Within a month all sections of the Mission were informed of this challenge by Mr. Stalley, the Field Director, and agreed to trust God for the money. So the contract was signed to purchase six months later by making a 60 percent payment. It is a thrilling story of seeing God supply step by step. With less than a month to go and still short $36,000, prayer was redoubled. Two more weeks passed with no appreciable increase. Then one day the telephone of the American office rang and a generous donor in past years inquired how things were going in Marseilles. Mr. Beacham, the Administrative Secretary, replied, "Just wonderful, we only need $36,000 more!" "Oh, very well," replied our friend, "I had already made out a check for $10,000. I'll just write another one for the same amount and send both along."

But that was not the end of miracles. When the day for the payment came, in March of 1967, although all the necessary money was in hand and had been transmitted to France, it had not yet reached the bank in Marseilles; such is the mystery of European financial transactions. But Mr. Gaston had to present himself to the official on that day anyway even if the deal fell through. However, an unexpected delay of a week required for the owner to procure a special permit which had previously been overlooked by the lawyer allowed sufficient time for the money from America to clear the bank and the deal was closed. In six months the remaining amount was paid and the former cheese factory became the home of the Radio School of the Bible approximately five and a half years after the work had begun in Tunis.

The distribution and reception of correspondence courses was not without its problems. To be sure, at the beginning it was possible to hand out applications wholesale as for example, at the International Fairs. Sometimes missionaries would stand outside schools and distribute BCC leaflets as hundreds of students passed by. At this time we were also operating several book stores and as missionaries made trips into the country distributing literature and selling books they took BCC leaflets with them. But little by little such liberty was curtailed until it finally came almost to a complete halt. Now it is only possible to give a piece of literature or sell a book to someone if it is requested. So this means you must learn how to turn a conversation to the desired subject and in such a way as to stimulate a request for what you have to offer.

But even in the beginning when the applications were filled out and mailed in requesting Bible lessons, there were still hazards ahead. Often someone in the family of the BCC student would recognize and confiscate the mail from RSB. People in North Africa do not receive anything like the volume of mail to which we are accustomed. Any piece of mail, especially one from France, is a big event in the home and is noticed by everyone. Sometimes the letter carrier himself would recognize the letter and destroy it. Once, the central Post Office of Algiers intercepted envelopes from Marseilles for several months and our correspondents received no word of any kind for a long time.When the postal authorities knew what those long brown envelopes with printed addresses and postage meter frank from Marseilles contained, it was easy to pull them all out and throw them away. What to do? Very simple, even if totally "un-American." Rather than use the efficient methods machinery permits we now distribute packets of letters and lessons to many volunteer groups in southern France so the envelopes, now white and of varying sizes, can be hand addressed and bear postage stamps. Thus the blockade was broken.

One protest in Casablanca backfired. A government official finding a BCC application blank (for the GMU in Malaga, Spain) wrote an article for the newspaper, Al-Alam, blasting the work of BCC as poisoning the youth of Morocco. He also sent the application blank with the letter as evidence. Accordingly, the newspaper published the article with a picture of the application blank on the front page. The result was that many people clipped out the picture from the newspaper and applied for the courses.

In many cases the BCC students used the address of a friend to avoid interception of the mail by their families. Frequently they met in the country or the woods to study together. Meeting together with friends also extended the ministry as a BCC student often would encourage his friend to apply as well. Learning this, the RSB staff then included several application blanks along with the lesson sheets in each subsequent letter. This almost invariably multiplied the number of new applicants.

But the most important thing was to keep a careful record of each applicant. When the first request was received the applicant was given a special file number and when the first lesson was returned an addressograph plate was made and a card filed. Thus a continuing record of his progress was kept. The general experience was that half of those first requesting BCC lessons never replied. From then on the number continued to drop until only about 10 percent followed through all the courses. Whenever a personal letter accompanied the lesson sheet it was answered personally. Even at this distance we knew we were dealing directly with people not just numbers. Often a regular personal correspondence ensued between the student in North Africa and a member of the RSB staff which permitted personal counselling. Such a contact is invaluable when the student has no Christian friend nearby to whom he can go for help or fellowship.

But what about the radio section. This, too, began in a small way; this time in Morocco. At about the same time that Voice of Tangier (now Trans World Radio) began with a studio high up on the mountain outside Tangier, we in NAM were considering the feasibility of radio ministry in North Africa. Later when Gordon Beacham visited the field for the International Council of 1959 he suggested to Don Harris that we start making broadcast tapes for transmission through ELWA. Years before Mr. Beacham had led in the development of SIM's first radio station, ELWA, in Liberia. This station had just built a new tower so they could beam towards North Africa. Mr. Beacham was eager to put the two together; our tapes over their antenna. Don Harris was at the time in SMM but merger plans between NAM and SMM were even then being worked out. Further, Don had received training in radio during his army service.

The Harris family was living in a noisy quarter of the big city of Marrakech, hardly the place for a recording studio. However, since the Mission was planning a rest station in the mountains for missionary holidays, it was decided to combine this station with the studio. At the same time Mr. G. Christian Weiss of Back to the Bible and formerly with GMU was looking for a project as a memorial to his recently deceased wife. So the Olga Weiss Memorial Studio of NAM took shape in the mountain village of Immouzer with Don Harris in charge and the NAM radio project was in operation.

As Moroccan citizens became aware that Gospel broadcasts were being sent out from within their country and in Arabic a strong reaction developed which forced TWR to transfer their facilities to Monte Carlo. The same pressures inclined NAM to move its studio from Immouzer. At the same time the Correspondence Course ministry was moving into its new quarters in the remodeled cheese factory in Marseilles. So it was decided to add the radio program and call the whole operation the Radio School of the Bible or *Ecole Radio Biblique* in French. After all, they are companion arms to the same program of evangelism and, complementing each other, should be coordinated.

The first thrust is radio; good, clear messages on a strong beam that can be easily tuned and understood. Then follow up the response to radio with a carefully prepared ministry through literature including, of course, systematic studies in the Bible. All of this comes under the head of primary evangelism, which is by no means an end in itself; merely the first step. It is extremely important to develop a person to person contact with the inquirer or serious student for without it few permanent results occur.

The strong conflict between Islam and Christianity has created such opposition to what Muslims consider rank heresy that the hostility of family and friends becomes a serious threat to any Muslim even considering Christianity as a personal option. It is therefore necessary for the inquirer to be helped to a clear understanding of the truth of the Bible message and the power of God to sustain a believer before he is prepared to make a valid decision for Christ. In fact, our experience has taught us two things about genuine conversions of Muslims in North Africa. If we expect the convert to stand fast and grow it will take a considerable period of thorough study. He also needs regular personal instruction, advice and encouragement from another Christian. It seems that not more than one in twenty Christians have reached a level of solid spiritual maturity without many hours of personal attention and help. Therefore, every effort is made to follow up the response to radio and the requests for correspondence courses with some personalized link. If at all possible, the respondent is put in touch immediately with either a national Christian or missionary in his neighborhood. Often the names and addresses of respondents are given to local Christians for follow-up. Failing this, an attempt to contact them personally is made by special persons from the RSB who regularly travel to North Africa in order to track down new contacts and renew fellowship by meeting old contacts, inquirers and Christians, where they live. Where even this is not possible, every effort is made to establish and maintain communication through personal correspondence from France. We are not dealing just with names or numbers. We are not interested in compiling impressive statistics. We are trying to reach people; individuals who need loving care and patient attention until they come to strong, healthy new birth in Christ. But our work or responsibility does not stop there. Then begins the often slow, agonizing period of spiritual childhood through adolescence to maturity.

For this reason several new departments were added to the RSB ministry in subsequent years; the *Key of Knowledge* magazine, the Theological Education by Extension (TEE) and the *Church Development Bulletin*. The *Key* (*Clef de la Connaissance* in French or *Miftah al Ma'arifa* in Arabic) was started as a humble effort with an edition of 10,000 in April, 1966. It consists of only four pages and is issued three times a year. But it is a good contact between RSB and both radio audience and correspondence students. In fact it serves as a link between these two ministries by advertising both in its pages. In addition there are stories illustrating Bible truths, Bible studies, personal testimonies of converted Muslims and a Readers' Corner where letters from interested persons are printed. Can you imagine what a joy it is for a North African to receive this little paper? We in the West get so much religious mail. We have so many Christian magazines. It is hard to appreciate what joy and blessing the *Key* brings to hundreds of isolated Christians. Moreover, until only a few years ago it was the only Christian periodical in the world for Arabic-speaking Muslims. Surely, this is a ministry worthy of developing into a larger form for more frequent issue.

Another missionary innovation, and this time from Latin America, Theological Education by Extension (TEE) has become a major ministry for church planting in North Africa. TEE developed in Latin America to meet the pressing need of giving advanced theological education to potential leaders in rapidly-growing churches who for family or business reasons, or both, could not leave their home to go any distance for schooling. The principle was very simple; student can't go to school—take school to the student.

As the age and level of education of the students taking our correspondence courses rose from high school to college and beyond we upgraded the lessons as well. At first they were very simple—almost too simple for school boys except for the fact that they dealt with ideas quite foreign, or even objectionable, to Muslims. Later, more detailed studies were added and even short surveys of the Old and New Testaments. But as better educated potential Christian leaders entered the ranks of Bible students there were two good reasons for going the TEE route.

First, simple Sunday school lessons will not train Christians to face the theological problems and make the theological decisions required for the leadership of Christian congregations in a world of subtle and violent attacks on the Bible and its teachings. Second, a class of men and women were becoming Christians who now qualified for this type of informed leadership and desired it. Specialized courses along these lines are given by the theological seminaries in the homelands. It is often the practice on some mission fields to send nationals to these foreign seminaries. However, years ago, the hazards of sending promising Christians abroad for theological training became painfully obvious; most potential leaders are not at liberty to leave home and go abroad to study and many of those who do go never return to take up leadership roles in their homeland. The next alternative was to start Bible schools or seminaries on the mission field. But even then the problem of leaving home even in one's own country to go to school still remained. And, in any case, the feasibility of operating such Christian institutions in independent Muslim countries seemed rather unlikely. The most practical alternative, therefore, seemed to be to develop a method to train gifted leaders right where they live and work.

The first steps taken were to encourage the missionaries to include "leadership training programs" in the summer camps. These programs at least provided better Sunday school teachers for the local worshipping groups; but not much more. Then some Navigator leaders visited our fields and held seminars on leadership under the heading "Studies in Christian Living." These proved so useful and welcome they were later translated into Arabic and French for wider distribution. Finally, we inaugurated a department in France to prepare TEE courses.

But all TEE programs are not pitched at the same level of education. I have seen some materials developed in East Africa and called TEE which were certainly not above grade school level. I suppose that by stretching definitions a bit, calling grade school Bible lessons theological education is justified, for they are, after all, about God or theology in the broadest sense. Generally, however, theological education refers primarily to post college, or at least, specialized training. Our courses, presently, are pitched at mid-college level. But they are still in the stage of early development. We can hardly keep ahead of our students year by year as we prepare new courses. Our plan is eventually to develop the courses for a full three year Bible college. The main reason for delay at the present time is the lack of qualified personnel. There is a need for persons capable of writing text materials in Arabic and French covering the basic elements of theology and Christian education so that these subjects will prepare students coming from the Islamic culture of North Africa to become competent leaders in the emerging national church.

Believe it or not, it is necessary to instruct our students, even in Lycee (high school plus) in the answers to destructive Higher Criticism. Some years ago, Abe Wiebe, then in Oran, Algeria, teaching some Algerian boys about Christianity sent out an S.O.S. His lessons were based on the assumption that the Bible, as God's Word, was trustworthy. But then the boys were being taught in school by French teachers that the Bible was just a collection of religious myths. So we must defend the Bible, in the face of Muslim opposition, from its foes in the nominal "Christian" camp. Furthermore, unfortunately, there are a few "missionaries" in North Africa of liberal theological persuasion. North African Christians must be warned and informed about these problems also. It is not enough that we must contest with Islam, Satan's cleverest distortion of Christian truth, but we must also contend with Catholicism and Protestant liberalism; and even, from time to time, with cults. So no matter if our Christian brothers and sisters in North Africa may be relatively strong and sincere they need and deserve the highest quality of Christian education available.

The TEE program centers in Marseilles where the courses are developed and the files are kept. Selected missionaries on the field act as tutors and Al Jessup, the Director, travels from Marseilles supervising instruction and helping to extend the program ever wider in North Africa where there are people anxious to get involved. As the national church grows we should see nationals assuming more and more responsibility in this ministry at all levels.

With specific relation to the developing Church, NAM instituted the *Church Development Bulletin* in 1968. This small periodical (now 20 pages per quarter, 8 inches x 6 and one-half inches) was started initially in order to coordinate missionary concepts and practices regarding the function and offices of the Church. In the early days of the Mission there was virtually no field supervision and missionaries conducted their work as taste and inclination led them. Of course at this time there was little or no vision for a truly national church and when worship was conducted or new converts added to local groups their qualifications for baptism or admission to communion were determined by the local missionaries. As could be expected, the standards of qualification for baptism or receiving communion regarding knowledge of Scripture or Christian lifestyle often varied significantly from station to station even when they were not many miles apart. This of course, tended to confuse everybody, missionary and national alike. Especially when one visited another city with different standards. Now, such confusing situations are unavoidable when different missionary societies or independent missionaries work in relative proximity. But surely, this kind of confusion ought not to exist when all the missionaries belong to one society. However, the necessary controlling factors are, first, a desire to agree to work together and, second, some structure to encourage cooperation. So when an active Field Administration was set up it then sought to collect the various plans and patterns for these functions of worship from across the field, study them in the light of Scripture, then establish uniform standards throughout the Mission. Such standardization requires considerable exercise of Christian grace and openness. But that, after all, is exactly what living in a Christian family in a Christian manner is all about. It is the true demonstration of interdenominationalism.

Initially, the purpose was simply to unify simple Christian standards for baptism and communion. Later as the worshipping groups grew in maturity and a desire for the exercise of some authority by nationals manifested itself, it became readily apparent that many more factors of Church life and function required study and dissemination. There are, in the first place, beliefs and practices in some groups which are not basically biblical. These must be isolated and prescribed. There are particular emphases of evangelical groups which must be identified and controlled. But there are also some basic biblical principles which can serve as general guidelines for groups of evangelical Christians as they seek to conduct themselves as local manifestations of the Church in North Africa. In recent years the Field Council, acting in behalf of the missionaries and the national Christians as well as possible, has sought through the pages of the *Bulletin* to serve as a clearing house for problems and questions regarding Church life as well as a source of unifying problems and tensions. And the proper spirit of Christian love and openness has smoothed the way and advanced the program. The *Bulletin*, latterly gives more space to questions of cultural contextualization and how the national church can grow to a responsible and recognized element in its home country.

Another product of these studies was a natural outgrowth of the preceding steps. A *Guide* was drafted in order to consolidate the results of the previous studies. As specially qualified persons applied themselves to research they then combined their conclusions into a document which could serve as a standard for church policy and administration across the field. This document was studied by all Councils of the Mission and was also submitted to outside experts for suggestions. The final draft then became the standard which was shared with the national Christians as a framework for the teaching and administration of the emerging churches.

THE ALGIERS MISSION BAND

God has used many different kinds of people to initiate service in pioneer areas of the world; clerks, soldiers, doctors, and teachers. In the case of what later became known as the Algiers Mission Band, it was the artistically talented daughter of a middle class Victorian family from London. Lilias Trotter early exhibited unusual artistic talent. In fact she took a few private lessons from the great artist-writer John Ruskin, who considered her to be his prize pupil and, with proper training, assured of a promising future as an artist.

However, at the same time, God was taking this highly sensitive English girl through a number of telling personal experiences which served to deepen her spiritual life and develop a compassionate desire to reach out to needy persons with her growing love for the Lord Jesus. This eventually led her to give her life in ministry to the Muslim people of Algeria.

A major formative experience was participation in the Dwight L. Moody meetings in London in 1875. She sang in the choir and worked in the counselling room. And this led her to initiate evangelistic and social work for the shop girls and, later, street walkers of London. Although she had a good place in society with many friends and every prospect for a successful career, a greater desire was growing in her heart, which she described in the following words, "To have His presence as a mere accompaniment for our lives will not now satisfy us. We must go His way with Him; it is the only path worth treading, when once our hearts come under His irresistible sway. And so the measure of sunshine and shadow in our days will be simply in the shining or the veiling of His face; nothing on earth will make up for the slightest dimming of that light; nothing will really matter that leaves it untouched."

Still God had wider horizons for Lilias Trotter than England. While she was fully occupied with her growing work in London with no thought whatever of anything like foreign missionary service, she came under the influence of two missionary ladies who seemed to her to have (in her own words) "taken to heart the outer darkness in a way I had not." She continues, "I saw that they had a fellowship with Jesus that I knew nothing about. So I began to pray, 'Lord, give me the fellowship with Thee over the heathen that Thou hast given these two.' "

Within weeks her prayer was answered. At a missionary conference in May, 1887, one of the first convened by the YWCA, Mr. Edward Glenny, a founding member of the NAM just six years earlier, spoke on North Africa. He began his address by saying that this was Thursday, and that on the Sunday before he was out on the Kabyle mountains (of Algeria) where Christ was unknown! With these words, God spoke to Lilias. By morning she was firmly convinced that God wanted her in Algeria.

In less than a year she and two companions arrived in the Bay of Algiers. It was a momentous and highly unconventional arrival. By their own admission they arrived, "none of us fit to pass a doctor for any society, not knowing a soul in the place, or a sentence of Arabic, or a clue for beginning a work on untouched ground: we only knew we had to come. Truly, if God needed weakness, He had it . . ." From this inauspicious beginning there grew a missionary band that at its height counted about thirty-five missionaries at a dozen localities, and lasted for over seventy years.

The character of the work was determined by the personality of its founder and her early associates. Since the founder was principally interested in women and children, they were always the main target in North Africa. Since the group started on the field without any administration in England, it was always a field-led group. In the absence of any sharply defined goal or strategy, the work grew as new towns and villages were visited and new recruits were posted.

Soon after arrival the three ladies leased a flat and hired a tutor in Arabic. The work was confined at first largely to personal contacts on the street and house visits. Then, lured by the hilltop villages just outside Algiers, they began to venture farther afield seeking the women and children they yearned to reach. Almost from the beginning literature distribution was a very important part of the ministry, even though few women, including those living in the cities, could read. In fact, due to Miss Trotter's unusual talents in both art and writing, the literature ministry of AMB grew to become its single most effective contribution to missionary work in the Arab world.

One missionary of the AMB, Harold Stalley, is of special interest due to his later service in NAM. Born in India to missionary parents, Mr. Stalley was well aware of the need for taking the Gospel to the non-Christian world. Many years later, while serving as a pastor in England, he was led to give serious consideration to the Muslim world, and Algeria in particular, by a book and a man. The book was Miss Trotter's well-known *Parables of the Cross*. In it the author draws lessons from the parables of Jesus which foreshadow His death. From the story of the "Corn of wheat" Miss Trotter drew the principle of spiritual power in the life of disciplined devotion which she summarized in the phrase *"Mors janua vitae"* which translated from the Latin means, "death is the gateway to life." This parable was fittingly and beautifully illustrated by some of Miss Trotter's exquisite drawings of plants and flowers. The whole message was tied into the ministry of the Gospel to Muslim people and emphasized the quality of personal spiritual life required to effect a fruitful witness to them. The man was Cecil Collinson at the time Chairman of the Home Council of the AMB. He was also a close friend and confidant, whom Mr. Stalley counted as a spiritual counsellor and father. As Mr. Stalley prayed about these leadings, asking God to clarify their meaning, he became increasingly convinced that he should offer for service in Algeria. His decision was confirmed in a remarkable manner. When he told Mr. Collinson of his intent, he learned that an elderly lady who had been saving up for years in order to take a Mediterranean cruise felt God say to her, just when she had accumulated sufficient money for the journey, "You are not to go; I want you to give this money to Mr. Collinson to send out a young missionary." His step of faith thus confirmed, Mr. Stalley went out to Algeria in 1934.

His introduction to North Africa and indoctrination into AMB was abrupt to the point of trauma. No candidate school, no missionary training center, no language school; it was like teaching someone to swim by tossing him immediately out of the boat into the water; sink or swim. Within two weeks of arrival the new young recruit was sent out to the desert villages with a Spanish colleague who knew French and Arabic but had only a few words of English. Mr. Stalley took up regular, if unprofessional, lessons in Arabic, as they travelled from village to village and was supposed to pick up French along the way. He eventually learned both languages, but was determined to improve the system if he ever got the chance which he did eighteen years later when he became Field Director of the NAM.

Five years after his arrival in Algeria World War II broke out. When the Germans invaded North Africa, Mr. Stalley was living in Tlemcen, in western Algeria. As an enemy alien the Vichy authorities placed him under house arrest. These were days of great hardship, which would have been much worse for the Stalleys and their small child if Algerian friends had not come to their rescue. During World War I, communications had remained open between England and North Africa, so that supplies and recruits, though diminished, still got through. This time, however, it was different. Relief only came with the arrival of the American troops after their landing at Oran.

Incidentally, one of the founding members of the newly-constituted American Council of the NAM in 1948, Mr. Edward Steele, was a naval officer with the forces which landed in Oran. But at that time, he knew nothing of the NAM nor of Mr. Stalley of the AMB.

For a short time the Stalleys worked for the Red Cross with the multitudes of service men. This was their first acquaintance with Americans, and, as he puts it, prepared him for years of close cooperation with the American "colonists" during the years of later international expansion of NAM.

Then it was home again to care for aging parents in England. While serving as a pastor in Bury-St. Edmonds in Suffolk, Mr. Stalley assumed the post of Home Secretary of AMB. During these years at home and with the perspective of distance, he began to ponder his field experiences and gradually reached several conclusions regarding changes which he thought might improve the work. First of all, he felt there should be a much greater proportion of men in order to reach a Muslim population more effectively. Second, the missionaries should be gathered in local teams of those whose talents complement each other, rather than to be scattered in ones or twos. Third, there should be a program for language study and cultural adjustment for the new recruits. In view of a serious fall-off in recruitment and seriously depleted forces in North Africa generally, he began to think about the feasibility of some plan for cooperation which would unite the Missions then serving in North Africa, and hence benefit all.

During his deputation ministry in England, Mr. Stalley made the acquaintance of Rev. Thomas Warren of NAM and, not long after, the Rev. Harold Fife with whom he shared his concerns. He found that both men had been thinking along similar lines. They agreed to work together for steps to implement these ideas. However, when the leaders of the SMM

and AMB were approached on the subject, they were not
favorably disposed and expressed the hope that in a short time
more recruits and funds would be forthcoming so that they
could continue on their own.

In time, this proved not to be the case, and eventually both
the SMM and the AMB were absorbed by the NAM. The
former still maintains a Council in Glasgow as an affiliate of
NAM, while the latter has been merged completely with the
English branch of NAM since 1965.

THE SOUTHERN MOROCCO MISSION

The history of the Southern Morocco Mission centers largely
on the names of three men: Anderson, Nairn and Haldane. It
was an extension of zealous evangelism generated in the south
of Scotland by the Alexander campaigns of the mid-nineteenth
century. As is usually the case, God raised up one man of
challenging personality to carry the evangelistic vision far
afield to a new and relatively untouched land. That man was
John Anderson.

Anderson was converted in 1859 at age 16 during the great
Alexander evangelistic campaign, and immediately threw
himself wholeheartedly into an intensive ministry of personal
evangelism. Early demonstrating his administrative gifts, he
founded and became the first president of the Ayreshire Christian Union, which was designed to organize earnest Christians
for spreading the Gospel throughout Scotland. In 1880 he
initiated a report of the Union's activities, which became a
regular periodical called *The Reaper*. Anderson lived and
worked at Ardrossan as a shipping agent, while supervising the
ACU, and continued in his own personal evangelistic efforts by
preaching and visitation.

In 1887, because of failing health, and following doctor's
orders to find a warmer climate that winter, John Anderson
took ship for southern Morocco. While he enjoyed and benefited
from the balmy climate with its warm sunshine, his sensitive
spirit was deeply disturbed by the great mass of Muslim people
in Morocco who were blinded by Satan and aliens to the grace of
God. While there, he met and talked with Mr. Edward Glenny,

founder of the NAM, who was in Tangier at the time. They discussed together the feasibility of sending some of the earnest Christians, products of recent evangelism in Scotland, to Morocco as missionaries. Mr. Glenny pointed out that due to the numbers of new recruits he was then handling for NAM, he could not see his way clear to receive any more from Scotland. He advised Anderson to consider sending recruits to the south of Morocco, promising to help them get located and provide facilities for language study. He suggested also that Mr. E. F. Baldwin, formerly with NAM presently living in Marrackech, would certainly be willing to help.

Strangely enough, upon his return to Scotland, Anderson seems to have gotten so deeply involved in other matters that plans for evangelizing Morocco were either forgotten or put aside. However, a serious decline in health, and a sickness which was nearly fatal, reminded him of his promise to God. So, upon recovery he immediately set about presenting his deep burden for Moroccan Muslims on every possible occasion. Not long thereafter, while speaking at a convention in Kilmarnock, Anderson challenged the Christians attending to consider the desperate need of people who had had no opportunity to hear the Gospel at all, and told them of his own yearning for the conversion of Moroccan Muslims. That night God touched the heart of a young farmer from Mauchline, who responded eagerly, and a few months later was on his way to Morocco. The young man was Cuthbert Nairn, who eventually spent 52 years as a missionary in South Morocco. His service was cut short by martyrdom in 1944.

The genius of John Anderson, however, had not run full course. In 1892, he became the first Principle of the Bible Training Institute in Glasgow. This school was started in order to provide systematic teaching of the Bible and other skills, to prepare competent Christian workers for the still growing evangelistic ministry in Scotland, as well as as for missionary service overseas. It is interesting to note that Anderson received this appointment at the recommendation of D. L. Moody, who was travelling in Scotland at the time. Anderson served in this capacity until 1914. However, since these additional responsibilities took up so much of his time, Anderson felt he could no longer continue to direct the affairs of SMM. So, that same year he assembled a group of men, who constituted the first Home Council of the Mission, and Cuthbert Nairn assumed leadership on the field. From 1888 until cessation of publication the ACU magazine, *The Reaper,* carried regular news about the SMM. When *The Reaper* closed in 1908, a special bimonthly magazine for the mission called *The Southern Morocco Mission* began and continued publication until the merger of the SMM with the NAM was effected in 1959.

After 13 years as Principal of the BTI, failing health led Anderson to locate in South Africa where, he maintained an active Christian witness. Later on, he returned to England and served fruitfully for several years as minister of the St. Andrew's Presbyterian Church in East London. Finally, however, his strength waned and he died in December, 1926, in his 84th year.

We now return to take up the history of that first missionary recruit of SMM, the young sheep farmer of Mauchline. Cuthbert Nairn was brought up in a strong Covenanter home "on porridge and the Catechism." As a boy, he was strongly affected by the testimony of the ACU evangelists who were travelling about the country taking meetings. But his conversion arose from the challenge of a student minister in the Free Church of Mauchline. He confirmed this decision privately the next morning while working in the barn. There was immediate evidence in his life of a genuine commitment to God. The young farmer became an ardent witness.

Special meetings for the deepening of the spiritual life were conducted by members of the ACU. At one of these in Kilmarnock, Nairn heard of the hopeless plight of Moroccan Muslims from John Anderson, who had only just returned from his visit to that country. The young man's heart was touched, and he volunteered on the spot to go as a missionary. Anderson, realizing how different life in Morocco was from life in Scotland, wisely urged Nairn to "count the cost." But the young man insisted that he felt God wanted him to go. After about two months acquainting friends with his decision, he sailed from London in December of 1888, accompanied by his sister, Jessie. They arrived in Mogador (now Essaouira) January 10th, the following year, and joined Mr. E. F. Baldwin, according to plan. In 1888 *The Reaper* carried an account of their departure for Morroco. The Nairns went out as representatives of the Ayreshire Christian Union since the SMM did not exist as yet. There is a further interesting paragraph which addresses questions regarding the propriety of sending out missionaries in this fashion, as follows: "We hear of sundry objections in certain quarters to our procedure in connection with this new departure in mission work. These may be summarized in these three queries: (1) why do we send out agents who have not gone through the usual college curriculum; (2) what will be done with the converts when there is no ordained minister to receive them into church fellowship? Some of our readers will think these objections are serious; others will feel doubtless amused. We shall try to answer them one by one. (1) We are sending out plain people because no B.D.'s or D.D.'s have offered. We heard a truehearted missionary lady say recently that she was proud of her noble-hearted husband who went out to China 22 years ago on one leg and crutches, because the men with two legs would not go! We commend this as sound reasoning, and we are acting on the same principle. We may add, however, our own conviction that anyone used of God to lead souls to Him in Scotland, is quite well fitted in ordinary circumstances for the same work in other lands. (2) We have not yet heard of any churches willing or prepared to take on mission work in this land. (3) What shall we say? We think our brother, Pastor Baldwin, will usually be within hail, but if not—what then? Will those whom God honors in the conversion of souls not be warranted to receiving them into church fellowship? Or would it be better that they should remain in their sins, rather than plan admission into the church of Christ by the hands of unauthorized laymen?"

The following paragraph spelled out the financial policy established at the very beginning: "We have had communication from a number of young men, offering themselves with willing hearts on His altar. But at the present moment, our way is not clear to accept more than the two friends, named above. We have no funds. We are led into this work by God, against our own intentions or wishes. Thus far, His leading has, in our judgment, been clear and unmistakable. But we cannot go faster or farther than He leads; if sufficient funds are sent in to warrant our engaging other missionaries, we shall certainly do so, and it is still our intention to make an effort as soon as circumstances will permit, to found a colony that will be self-supporting."

Immediately upon arrival in Essaouira, the Nairns plunged into language study. Almost before they could handle more than a few phrases of Arabic, both were out witnessing, Jessie in nearby homes, and Cuthbert farther afield as they travelled with Mr. Baldwin. After a short time, they moved a hundred miles inland to Marrakech, in those days a four day journey by muleback.

Within six months of the Nairns' arrival in Morocco, three more recruits went out from London. Actually, there were more than a dozen applicants by this time, but due to upset conditions in Morocco, only three were sent out. Year after year, new recruits were added until the missionary force numbered more than 20 persons, nearly all single.

Particular aspects of Muslim society in Morocco indicated the advisability of having married couples in charge of each station. So the Council acknowledged the need for couples. Consequently, three weddings among the missionaries took place in 1893, and three years later Cuthbert Nairn, himself, was married. By this time, the four main centers of SMM had been established and staffed. They were Mogador (Essaouira), Mazagan (El Jadida), Marrakech (sometimes earlier called Morocco City) and Safi. Later, Azemmour, Agadir and Taroudant were added.

Literacy was not widespread among the Moors at this time, especially in the rural areas. But medical and health needs were enormous. This fact led SMM to seek medical personnel and locate dispensaries in strategic places, from which itineration and colportage could fan out. Some of the missionaries were fully qualified doctors. Others, as essentially lay persons, got special training; some in Scotland, some with the NAM in its hospitals and the rest with Mr. Baldwin.

Mr. Nairn, for example, spent virtually his whole time of service in Morocco at the dispensary in Marrakech. And it was

here, on the 9th of November, 1944, he was stabbed in the back
by a demented man and died, after 55 years of service. In some
respects, this was a fitting end to the service of a man who had
written upon his arrival in Morocco, "It means we must be
willing to experience Gethsemanes, bitter sorrow and have
fellowship with Christ in His sufferings, and that we be willing
to labor day and night with tears. The flesh shrinks from such a
course, but the fire is burning, and as eternal things become
more real, the things of time are fading from our sight." In fact,
his Scripture verse for that fatal day was Philippians 1:19,
"Unto you it is given in behalf of Christ, not only to believe on
Him but also to suffer for His sake." Truly, he enjoyed the
privilege of suffering for His Saviour's sake. Nairn's last letter,
received in Scotland a few days after his death, was almost
prophetic. In it, he said,

> In speaking of the difficulties of work in a Mo-
> hammedan land, I do not mean to say that none have
> been saved, by all the past years of seed sowing.
> There are those now in the presence of the King, who
> can sing the song of Moses and the Lamb, and there
> are those living around us now who rejoice in Jesus
> as their Saviour. So let us be glad and press on. How
> much easier it will be for young workers who come
> out now. Weary days of travel on muleback have
> given way to the speedy car. Language study has
> been simplified by a suitable course prepared for new
> workers. As they preach the Gospel, they will not be
> met by dull, vacant looks, because it is now so
> well-known in general. But more than all, they can
> expect to enter upon the joyful work of reaping what
> others have sown. God's time may be very near.
> "Due season is in His control." That season may be
> theirs, and what they reap from our sowing will but
> provide everlasting rejoicing for us all. Come over
> then and help us. Listen to the words of a great
> missionary: "henceforth there is laid up for me a
> crown of righteousness." The same crown is waiting
> for us, too, if we hasten His coming by our faithful
> obedience to His great commission to preach the
> Gospel to every creature. Amen.

The third man God raised up as a major leader in the SMM was James Haldane. He was born in the Perthshire village of Auchterarder, just three years before the first missionaries of the Ayrshire Christian Union arrived in Morocco. He was converted by the witness of a lady who conducted special classes for a few boys to supplement the education provided in the village. This, together with his association with the Mission Hall of the village, taught him to know and love Christ. It also appears that these early years established him in a firm trust in the sovereignty of God from which he never wavered, and which stood him in good stead during the trying days of his later service in Morocco.

By 1906 he was a student at the Bible Training Institute (B.T.I.), Glasgow. It was here that he first came in contact with the SMM, since under John Anderson's leadership the office of the Mission was located in the B.T.I. building, now on Bothwell Street.

However, upon completing his studies, interest in Morocco seems to have waned, for he took ship to Newfoundland. If Morocco was the "Nineveh" of his call, perhaps Newfoundland was his "Tarshish." At any event, he returned to Scotland after a year, then set out for Morocco near the close of 1912. Nancy Carlisle, another SMM recruit on board, became his wife three years later. Shortly after beginning his studies of Arabic with Cuthbert Nairn, he wrote home, "When passing village after village along this road, it is impossible to feel otherwise than sad, when it is remembered that they are without a single missionary of the Cross. Starting in the early morning on horseback, one can see the smoke from scores and scores of villages, lying in darkness, untouched by the Grace of God."

Haldane, a keen student of languages and culture, made this comment during his later years, "It's not sufficient to learn merely the language of the people among whom we live and work; we must also study to understand their traits embedded in their character, which color their words and give them a significance, not always apparent on the surface. Failure to do this will inevitably lead us into entanglements and perplexities which can have no other effect than that of damaging the very work we are eager to accomplish."

In contrast to Nairn, who operated a clinic in one location, Haldane was always seeking new frontiers. He was challenged by the innumerable villages spread across the wide plain and up the valleys at the foot of the mountains, and planned to reach as many as he could. In fact, he kept right on at this program of itineration up through World War II. Finally, the family returned home in 1951 to settle near their son in England.

Two elements predominated in Haldane's mind: a sharply clear Gospel of God's gracious provision for depraved sinners, utterly devoid of ambiguity or compromise, and a sense of dogged determination in the face of indifference and obstacles, confident that obedient service for a Sovereign God is never fruitless. There are indications that he was probably a little difficult to get on with. Determined men of spirit usually are. But he was committed to biblical principles to a degree often lacking among missionaries today.

Nevertheless, Haldane made two penetrating predictions which we would do well to observe today. They both spring from his firm convictions regarding the kind of servant needed and service possible under constant, strong opposition through the power of a Sovereign God. Writing on the subject of candidate qualifications in an article entitled, "Sit Down; Count the Cost," he discussed the reasons, as he saw them, for dropouts and brief service among missionaries to Morocco. Referring to the Lord's parable concerning discipleship in Luke 14, he said, "Our Lord would not accept service offered on the impetus of emotion, held alone by nothing more than a desire for change. Those who would follow Him must know at the start that service in the Kingdom means sacrifice, a leaving of all and following Him. Failure on the Mission field can often be traced to the fact that the candidate had not counted the cost; his eagerness has outstripped his calculations of the sacrifice involved. It is not when we are in a ferment of emotion, nor when we are hankering after a line in life that will skip the daily monotony that irritates us, that we should judge ourselves fit for the missionary task, but rather at our desks where, by sober calculation, we may come to know what correspondence exists between our resources and those of the enemy we are to challenge."

Furthermore, it seems that Haldane had an unusually clear
concept of the purpose of missions being to extend the Church.
Writing nearly fifty years ago he said, "The formation of an
aggressive, Christian church in this land is held up by Islam's
tyrannous denial of religious liberty to those who desire to
make a break with a system which works no deliverance and
gives no peace. In circumstances such as these, we must not
hurry to hurl the epithet of 'coward' against men and women
whose difficulty in the way of open confession can hardly be
exaggerated. At this juncture, it would be unwise, we think, to
urge converts to a form of evangelization which, by reason of its
aggressiveness, would lead to open conflict with both the
political and religious bodies of the country. The time is not yet
ripe, but to achieve our end which will lead to widespread and
open preaching, and upon which the evangelization of the
people depends, our first step is to form churches wherever
possible, however small. In some towns, such groups already
exist. As their number grows and the feeling of fellowship
becomes deeper and intensified, there will come to some of these
converts at least an experience of Divine fullness, which by its
overflow will reach outside it and demonstrate its reality and
patient self-denial and so create the atmosphere where a more
aggressive testimony for Christ becomes possible."

He also clearly stated his determination to stick at the job, in
spite of limited visible results in terms of his convictions that
obedience to God is more important than statistics which
impress men. However, he had not settled for fruitlessness, nor
was he prey to frustration. Frankly admitting meager results,
he summarized his first eleven years of service by reporting,

> If I tell you that the majority of Moroccans to
> whom I have preached the Gospel all these years are
> as firmly attached to their false prophet as they were
> when I first met them, it is a fact which should excite
> further prayer and effort, rather than a fact which
> should be allowed to extinguish our faith. No doubt,
> some of our friends at home find our reports dull at
> times, but let them remember—our standard is high,
> and our ministry unstained either by the attraction

of compromise or the weakness of concession. Until the Moroccans are willing to snap the last link of their faith in Mohammed and receive Christ, we refuse to register them as converts. Remember the log book of Columbus, full pages of it were filled with three words: "Just sailed on." The same weary waste of waters, sailors clamoring for a return to their country, weeks without a single incident to break the monotony—"just sailed on." But at last they furled their sails, and let go anchor in a new world! Let us, in our sphere, go and do likewise.

Such vision and faith are sorely needed today.

The SMM never became a large mission. At its height just after 1900, there were up to 20 missionaries. The number dwindled to under ten through the early 1950's, and rose again for the last five years before merger to about 15. The scope and character of the work remained more or less uniform. Based on a half dozen stations, emphasizing a medical ministry combined with the distribution of literature and seizing every opportunity for personal witness and Bible study, several score earnest Christians, mostly from Scotland, labored to make Jesus Christ known savingly to the Muslims of Southern Morocco.

When in 1959 it was deemed advisable to link forces with the NAM, an agreement was reached which while putting field affairs under the supervision of the merged Mission retained the office in Glasgow in order to continue representing the needs of North Africa to the people of Scotland. This agreement was formalized on the field at a special ceremony following the International Council meeting in 1961.

5

LOOKING AHEAD

"LET US RISE UP AND BUILD...."

Nehemiah was motivated for a cause which he recognized as God's and with which he completely identified. His first concern, however, was to share this burden 'to rebuild' with his brethren. And it was then that the real miracle took place in the hearts of the people through a transfer of vision. A challenge to rebuild a wall became a collective goal for they responded to Nehemiah saying, 'Let us rise up and build.' This is what needs to happen through the ranks of the North Africa Mission, its supporters and praying constituency; a transfer of vision that binds hearts and hands together for God's cause and glory.

Abe Wiebe
International Council
1975

EVALUATION

After a century of Protestant missions in North Africa, it would seem a good thing to evaluate the performance of the past in order to improve for the future. There is always room for improvement. Moreover, the world missionary movement has suffered a period of "imperialism" and is struggling with more or less success to achieve partnership with the growing national churches. In North Africa we are just now witnessing the emergence of the national church and are grappling with the problems of partnership. It seems to me we ought to be able to learn from our own mistakes in the past, as well as from the mistakes of others who faced similar problems. Then as we plan for the future we ought also to be able to profit from the mistakes of missions in non-Muslim areas where the work is far in advance of ours.

The theology and practice of missions have passed through many stages of refinement since the ardent William Carey had his vision for the conversion of Indians put down by the remark of a church official, "Young man, if God desires the conversion of the Indian people, He can do it without your help." In recent years a new method has been advocated to supplant the old-fashioned practice of sending missionaries out from the western so-called Christian countries to the unevangelized fields. "Reach foreign visitors in your country while they are away from home; then they will go back and evangelize their own people." Intriguing; but fallacious. Reaching foreign nationals in our homeland is a worthy concept and a natural expression of Christian concern for their spiritual well-being. But evangelism of foreign guests in our homelands must never become a substitute for sending out missionaries. It just does not work that way.

But now let us go back to the early stages of missionary work in North Africa and trace the development from that point. We can easily recognize changes and improvements as we move forward with the development from that first small beginning in the hills of Kabylia. It will also be instructive to compare the work of the NAM with that of other groups working in the same general area at the same time, for it must be recognized that the

NAM did not work alone in North Africa. We have already seen that the American Methodist Episcopal Church labored for nearly seventy years in Algeria and Tunisia. Their work is considerably reduced at the present time and is confined to Algeria. Then there were the two small British missions, Algiers Mission Band and Southern Morocco Mission, which were later absorbed by NAM. But there were also others. Chief among these is the Gospel Missionary Union which worked in Morocco. The GMU began in 1894 when a party arrived in Morocco at the invitation of Mr. Glenny. Incidentally, the seeds of interest in North Africa which led to the founding of GMU had been sown some five years earlier by Dr. Grattan Guinness when he lectured at a Summer Bible School in Kansas. The GMU worked more in rural areas, emphasized the colloquial dialect of Arabic and conducted camps and conferences. They initiated Bible correspondence courses, produced much literature and helped get radio programs started. Most of their people were expelled after Moroccan independence, and they operate from Malaga, Spain today. There have also been missionaries from the Plymouth Brethren, the Anglican Church Missionary Society and several other smaller groups. Since nearly all the groups were theologically congenial, we all worked together in harmonious fellowship. The NAM, as the largest of all and the only mission working in all three countries had the responsibility to coordinate programs and encourage cooperation in various projects.

As we engage in this review we must remember the nature of the times and the spiritual climate of that day which gave rise to the so-called "faith missions," since that name has been called into question many times in subsequent years as not being really appropriate. However that may be, in the beginning it was accurate.

For several decades following the Spiritual or Evangelical Awakening of 1859 in Great Britain thousands of Christians of all denominational persuasions were driven by the Holy Spirit to deeper personal commitment to Jesus Christ through Bible study and prayer. These committed Christians then found the ties of spiritual fellowship across denominational lines stronger than the bonds of their denominational communities. They also found great blessing through service in Christian organizations which spanned denominational boundaries. So it was not long before the new evangelical organizations at home saw counterparts in similar organizations engaged in overseas missions. Thus the genesis of the so-called faith missions. They had no organized church budget or constituency upon which they could depend. Their tangible support came from devoted Christians from different denominational groups whom God had led together to open up new fields for service. In the main this was a good thing; people moved by the Spirit of God gave expression to their new-found enjoyment of the blessing of God in practical dedicated service. To the degree that it encouraged too strongly a spirit of independence there were dangers. Enthusiasm does not always produce practical results. When personal individualism is interpreted as spiritual guidance at the expense of the clear biblical pattern of order and discipline, problems arise. Many small individualistic efforts at foreign missions aborted due to instability. But many struggled through trying birth-pains and continued.

There have been criticisms of several aspects of the interdenominational groups by people of denominational persuasion. And many of these criticisms are indeed valid. For example, it has been said that by and large, the relatively unstructured interdenominational societies lacked adequate discipline and direction, had a vague concept of ecclesiology and seemed not to appreciate the significance of the sacraments. On the other hand, the denominational society came with its own structure and, according to clearly developed plans, planted a church; albeit its own (foreign) church in the new country.

There is a basic confusion of ideas here. Even if it is true, very largely, that the earlier faith missions in North Africa were rather loosely organized and did not seem to have had as a clear, commonly accepted goal the planting of a church, it does not follow that a denominational organization whose program is to plant churches of foreign culture and structure in the newly evangelized country is following the biblical pattern of building strong national churches. The most cogent statement of the case for denominational groups in North Africa can be found in a book by W. N. Heggoy, a Methodist missionary to North

Africa,* even if denominational bias does show through. As the only scholarly history of Protestant missions in North Africa this book is invaluable.

Even if it is simpler to transport a foreign church to the mission field that does not make it right. Surely, by now, having struggled through the throes of adjustment first to the concept of indigenuity, then the "three-self movement" and, even more recently, the still not clearly or commonly understood process of "contextualizing," the program of exporting a foreign ecclesiastical entity together with its hierarchy, liturgy and structure to an entirely new culture should be seen as unwarranted, unnecessary and perhaps also, unacceptable procedure.

It seems to me that the path of truth lies somewhere between these two extremes; largely unstructured, on the one hand, and overly structured on the other. So let us first consider the criticisms levelled at the undenominational groups by denominational spokesmen and then we can examine the denominational program. First of all, there is the definition of terms. As opposed to the denominational society which exports itself overseas there is the un-, or non-, or inter-denominational society whose membership is drawn from different denominations but which does not impose any particular denominational structure on the emerging church overseas. (In point of fact, however, nearly every mission of this type known to me personally is essentially baptistic as opposed to paedobaptistic in practise.) Curiously, Heggoy states that the Methodist Episcopal Mission in North Africa could be called "interdenominational" because it included members of other denominations. But then he adds that ultimately all members of the Mission had to join the Methodist Episcopal Church and come under its jurisdiction, which does not really sound "interdenominational" to me.

Now, however, we come straight to the criticisms levelled at the non-denominational groups. And we must remember that these criticisms arise from a study of the actual operations of several groups in North Africa, especially the NAM. So it is important to face each criticism frankly to determine its validity. And then we can see if perhaps some of the mistakes or

* Fifty Years of Evangelical Missionary Movement in North Africa, 1881-1931, *by W.H. Heggoy.*

weaknesses of the first fifty years have since been corrected. In order to distinguish clearly between the two different kinds of missionary operations in North Africa, Heggoy defines two types; the Band and the Team. He describes the Band as characteristically exhibiting a lack of organization and planning. On the other hand he calls a group with organization and coordinated planning, a Team. He groups NAM with AMB and GMU under the classification of Bands as contrasted with the Methodist mission as a Team and concludes that as a result of the tighter church-oriented structure of the latter, there was closer supervision and direction of field activities. This direction, he says, also led to the development of a greater variety of programs for different age groups including efforts at basic education where permitted. But the main point is that working from within a clearly defined church structure, the Methodists deliberately set about selecting, training and ordaining converts as pastors who would give proper emphasis to and exercise administration of the sacraments. Surveying the work of NAM, AMB, GMU, etc., Heggoy quotes from AMB their declared strategy in its simplest terms; dispersion and distribution. That is to say, scatter the missionaries everywhere you can across the field and then encourage them to disperse even more widely by village visitation until as many people have been contacted as is humanly possible, albeit with little deliberate effort to sustain anything like a regular follow-up program. In connection with this kind of dispersion of personnel there was also apparently the practice of missionaries moving from place to place as they saw fit. The wide dispersion of missionaries, however, did achieve a wider distribution of literature than otherwise possible. And the sale of Bibles and offer of booklets and tracts was indeed a major factor in missionary activity. The lack of concentration, however, did hamper the development of stable groups.

Another contrast noted by Heggoy is the greater number of places with resident missionaries reported by the Bands than the Team. But he points out that often only two or three persons were located at one place and there was frequent changing of personnel, often leaving once occupied places vacant for long periods of time. He makes an arbitrary but useful distinction between "posts," occupied from time to time by relatively few and changing personnel, and "stations" better staffed with missionaries of varied skills and therefore supplementary programs. By and large the Bands had "posts" while the Team established "stations."

While there is some justification for these distinctions and the criticisms which they suggest, the case has been somewhat overstated. Naturally, a denominational organization will work more closely to a fixed pattern since it has imported the closely defined home structure and will develop its work there along the same lines. Moreover, the AMB was indeed a loosely structured group with a rather broad program of visitation and literature distribution, now and then supplemented by simple Bible instruction. Being largely a women's society without any explicitly declared strategy beyond evangelism, little thought was given to anything like church planting. It did therefore consitute a distinctly different pattern from that of the Methodists. It is only fair to note, however, that in later years AMB operated more from fixed bases. However, the NAM, at least as early as 1894, had declared as its objective, "to see raised up in North Africa self-sustaining and self-propagating communities of regenerate men and women." Furthermore, Mr. Glenny's frequent trips to the field gave NAM a sense of direction most other groups lacked. Nevertheless, it does not seem that there was any clearly defined goal as to what form those "communities of regenerate men and women" would take and, therefore, apparently there was no definitely designed systematic program laid out to achieve that goal. Perhaps the hope was that as converts were made and then given some general Bible training, little groups of Christians originally meeting with the missionaries at their invitation and in their houses would gradually assume more and more leadership until these little assemblies were eventually under the control and direction of North Africans. In short, it may well have been the view of the Bands that the local church should be developed by converted North Africans rather than be superimposed upon them as was the program of the Team. In any case, by 1978 there still was no such thing as a truly independent church of converted Muslims anywhere in North Africa.

But now, after all these years, a truly national church is emerging at last. Why has it taken so long? In the first place, it was not until missions had been active for years, even decades, all around the world that the production of a national church was seen as the biblical goal of missionary work. Even then mission leaders often classified some areas or countries as too resistant to the Gospel for any real expectation of founding churches there. Among areas or countries considered unlikely to produce churches were those that were largely or totally Muslim in religion or culture. Though in some of these, as for example, Egypt, a nearly dead national Christian church, which was a survival of one of the ancient churches of past history, often found new spiritual life through the witness of foreign missionaries. But, so far as North Africa is concerned, since there is no survivor of an ancient church, the goal of missions had always been a national church made up of converts from Islam which would be able to run its own affairs and carry its own witness independent of any outside help. And we are just now reaching that goal.

In spite of the fact that no clear plan was made to establish a national church, in the early days, some effort was made to gather inquirers and those professing faith for a time of study and worship. And in a true sense these gatherings were expressions of the Church. In fact if only a handful of missionaries alone met for worship they alone constituted, however small, the Church in that location. But a truly independent national church is quite another matter.

It is interesting, however, to note a comment made in the magazine *North Africa* (1934 pg. 2) regarding a meeting of Arab men in Tangier. "God has wonderfully blessed some of the young men and they are taking part in speaking and prayer with general acceptance. Last Sunday two of these conducted the whole service with manifest grace from the Lord. Special prayer is needed that what is undoubtedly the beginning of a real indigenous Church of converted Moors may be preserved and guarded by God from all that would harm it." A little too optimistic, perhaps, since the Arab meeting in Tangier never did actually become an indigenous church. But it evidences a vision for one. Doubtless such promising groups appeared at many other places across North Africa over the years but for one reason or another—inadequate national leadership, dispersal or departure of mature Christians, pressure of outside forces or even lack of vision on the part of the missionaries—none ever became a truly independent group of converts which would be accurately described as a national church. Apparently the vision and hope was not sufficiently united to expectation and a definite program vigorously pursued to culmination.

Little by little as the field forces were more closely coordinated by a Field Director and he began to lay out particular steps in a plan to prepare for indigenous churches, we find regular consideration of this subject by the International Council. The plan took two forms. First, develop the tools which will help local national Christians and missionaries to carry out programs preparatory to a national church. These consisted of special guidelines regarding the qualifications for becoming a member of the church and for the administration of the sacraments. Second, look out for men of spiritual maturity evidently possessed of the gifts of leadership and help them get the necessary further training so they can exercise those gifts properly. This led to the addition of a series of courses in TEE to the curriculum of BCC, and also to the drafting of a Guide by the Field Council to ensure that uniform policies were being followed at every station.

Furthermore, missionaries and nationals initiated conversations regarding the steps they thought would advance the appearance of the national church. I remember hearing a Moroccan leader say, "I wonder when a score or more Moroccans will be led of God to band together as members of the Christian Church, demand recognition from the government and be ready to pay the price such a stand may require." When more North African leaders begin thinking along these lines, we will see steady progress.

Unfortunately, but understandably, there were times of tension between national Christians and missionaries; just as between adolescent children and parents in even the best of families. Having discovered that they really could and should become increasingly independent of their elders and having accepted more responsibility to make more decisions, they

began to chafe against real or imagined restraints and throw
their weight around a bit. On their part, the elders (the
missionaries) sometimes tended to overreact and add to the
confusion by talking about relinquishing, not only their
authority over the church, but also over legitimate Mission
concerns also. However, with time came the wisdom of moderation and a relaxing of tensions on both sides. What a tragedy it
would have been if the very event which we had been praying
about for so long should come to be seen as a threat rather than
a triumph! I do not know which proverb fits best; "Don't throw
out the baby with the bath water" or "Don't crack eggs with a
hammer." But certainly moderation, patience and love were
needed. Fortunately, after some brief adjustments to a new and
wonderful relationship, a healthy and responsible partnership
has developed which augurs well for the future.

Some years ago a heteregeneous group including three
Algerians acquiesced in a plan sponsored by the World Council
of Churches and lent their names to an organization called the
Algerian Christian Church. But this church existed solely on
paper and soon vanished into thin air. It has been noted that
the Methodists ordained several Algerian pastors, but they
seem to have functioned chiefly under the direction of the
Methodist missionaries and the churches, such as they were,
amounted to a small group of Europeans and North Africans
meeting on mission property. Whatever they were they have
since disappeared. This raises serious question whether, in fact,
the vaunted Methodist scheme was as effective as it claimed to
be.

Dr. Heggoy points out from his perspective of 1960 that both
the Bands and the Team based their hopes on two fallacious
assumptions. The first was that it would be wise to work with
European citizens of North Africa in order through them to lay
a foundation for or, at least, create an atmosphere conducive to
the development of a national church of converted Muslims.
Time soon proved such hopes to be in error. In fact, rarely
anywhere in the world does a Christian group of non-Muslims in
a Muslim country constitute a nucleus for the formation of a
church attractive to Muslim converts. Rather, in almost every
case the reverse is true; especially if the Christian group in the

Muslim country represents a survival of the earlier Church of bygone days. It is like trying to mix oil and water.

The second fallacy was the assumption that since the Berbers were the indigenous peoples in the land and were Islamized by invading Arabs, these Berbers ought to be easier to reach since their Islamization was, perhaps, not so deepseated as that of the invaders. This too proved false. Often individuals or groups newer to Islam, or even only superficially Muslim, are the more obdurate. At any rate, when Morocco, Algeria and Tunisia became independent countries their governments have systematically pushed Arabic Islam at the expense of the native Berber culture.

However, it was the declared purpose of the Mission from the start to work among the Kabyle Berber people. A few years later "and the other Berber peoples" was added to the Mission's name in order to include the Chaouia of eastern Algeria with the Riffi and Schleuh of Morocco. The thought underlying this concept was that since the Berber people were indigenous to North Africa they, as the basic people, should be the main target of evangelism with the hope that they would become the foundation for a Christian people in North Africa.

It was not long before the work of the Mission was expanded to include the Arabic population and also the various groups of Europeans. First of all, the Arabic population was heaviest in the large cities and easier to reach than Berbers. Secondly, French suspicion of and opposition to the efforts of "English spies"—as the NAM missionaries were often designated—was much greater when those "spies" were wandering around among the rural areas and villages of the Berbers. So for one reason or the other, even today, little work and less fruit has resulted from efforts to reach Berbers and establish a national Christian witness in the Berber culture and language. In fact, right now the Arabization program of the government of Algeria has led them to view with suspicion any emphasis on Berber work as an effort to encourage the development of Berber culture as alien to their desire to create a unified Algerian (Arabic) culture.

A word about Arab versus Berber with reference to North Africa would probably be helpful in clarifying the situation there. Strictly speaking there are actually very few pure Arab people in North Africa. Their physical appearance bears this out. True Africans have rounder faces. And pure Berbers can scarcely be distinguished in appearance from the people of Southern Europe. There is much Berber blood in the total population of North Africa even among those whose language and culture is Arabic. And there are also millions of virtually pure Berbers in the country and mountain areas still retaining their distinctive language and culture. However, the governments of all three countries consider themselves to be part of the Arab world and they are emphasizing this fact in their political and cultural relations.

Nevertheless many of the strongest Christians today in North Africa have come originally from Berber background and are proud of their Berber roots, although they have been assimilated into the general Arabic culture of their countries. So although the internal tension between Berber and Arab remains to a certain degree, missionaries as guests in the country should not get involved in it lest they jeopardize their relations with the government.

It is interesting to note the way the Lord prepared the NAM for the development of independence in North Africa. We have seen that at first the thrust was toward the Kabyles of Algeria. Then interest developed in other Berber tribes. But at the same time almost from the beginning some missionaries worked among Europeans and even the Jewish communities. Before long most of the work was conducted through Arabic with French as the second language—with the exception of Libya where Italian was used and northern Morocco where Spanish was common.

In 1951 at the International Council, however, the NAM decided to phase out the European work and concentrate in Arabic with French as an auxiliary language. That same year Libya became independent followed five years later by Tunisia and Morocco and six years afterward by Algeria. Since the rebirth of the Church in North Africa has always been our goal and that Church, as a truly indigenous Church, must be made up of nationals who virtually without exception would be converts from Islam, it was wise strategy to concentrate on the target group.

What conclusion, then, can be drawn from this review of the past? Is the Team approach to be preferred over the Band? Is it possible for the Team to encourage the development of a truly national church along its own cultural lines? New denominations have been springing up throughout the course of history. So long as they follow the basic principles of biblical theology one is as Christian as the other in spite of secondary differences. But the question facing foreign missions is whether to impose on the newer, younger Christians all the denominational differences and distinctives together with their tensions and problems, which are a product of European history since the Reformation. Why not just teach basic biblical principles for salvation and the Christian life and then let the national Christians develop their own ecclesiology? And, is it realistic to think along these lines?

Ideally, we would like to see one national church grow in North Africa with the necessary separate branches in each of the three countries. There are few enough Christians as it is without further dividing them into small denominational groups. No matter what agency God used to bring North Africans to faith in Christ, they need each other and would be strengthened by joining together in one church. However, this dream, though undeniably biblical, may prove to be unrealistic due to the presence of missionary groups in North Africa which have come from separate home denominations. Past history teaches that such groups always propagate their distinctive home structures and identities. We would hope that at least all groups will be sound theologically and open for fellowship and mutual assistance.

To this end, then, there must be materials and facilities for the propagation of the Gospel, instruction of converts and training of leaders. Much more is needed at this level right now. Correspondence courses, the Visualized Bible, Theological Education by Extension, etc., are still in the beginning stages. There is virtually nothing available in the broad field of Christian literature; teaching materials, commentaries, Bible study helps, books on the family and society from the Christian standpoint and so forth; let alone periodicals covering various aspects of Christian living in a hostile world. In order to produce these materials we need trained Christian theologians and writers. Some materials are available from Christian Arab sources in other parts of the world, but newer, local productions are necessary also.

The problem of providing adequate training facilities at all levels meets governmental restrictions head on. So long as the local governments can perpetuate the fiction that there are no genuine national Christians it will be easy to prohibit the development of training facilities for a foreign and objectionable religion. However, when a significant minority of national Christians comes into being there will be leverage to get the government to recognize the legitimate rights of that group according to the provisions of their constitutions; as in Nigeria where there is a strong, ruling Muslim majority but also a strong, if smaller, Christian minority.

In the meanwhile, as the national church grows, our partnership role will also grow and we must seek ways to encourage and support the development of national leadership.

MARTYRS IN NORTH AFRICA

It is appropriate to speak of "martyrs of the faith" and indeed such Christians deserve notice; primarily as examples of believers who because of their personal trust in God would not compromise, alter or deny their relationship to Jesus Christ the Saviour who died for them on the Cross. The strength that enabled them to withstand the pressure of persecution whether subtle or violent was their confidence in the companionship and power of the resurrected Redeemer they knew they would one day see face to face.

However, there is some confusion over the use of the term "martyr." To whom does it refer; any Christian who dies suddenly or unexpectedly or violently in a foreign land? Or, must a Christian have suffered death unmistakably because of his Christian faith in order to be considered a martyr? Suppose a Christian goes to a strange land in order to introduce the Gospel and while there dies as a result of political violence or accident, or even disease, should that death be called martyrdom?

Let us look first at the basic meaning of the word. Fundamentally, "martyr" means "witness," both as a noun and a verb. Later, because so many Christians suffered from a violent reaction to their witness the word took on a narrow more specialized meaning "to suffer and especially to die because of the witness." And this derived meaning is the common meaning of the word today.

If the word "martyr" be restricted to those who die beyond any doubt because the resentment to their Christian faith produced a violent reaction ending in death, then there have been very few missionary martyrs among national believers. However, I believe that the scores of missionaries from Britain who deliberately exposed themselves to disease and malnutrition, among other things, out of a love for the Lord Jesus and a desire to make Him known to Muslims and died because of it qualify as martyrs also.

What we must avoid is exaggerating the role of martyrdom to the point of sensationalism which distracts from the glory of God and emphasizes the virtue of man. The important element in martyrdom is that the Christian was willing to suffer death if necessary and did not shrink from it when it seemed imminent; not just that he died. I do not doubt that there have been many involuntary martyrs whom death snatched away before they knew what was happening; and also many brave Christians who suffered terribly yet upon release escaped martyrdom.

Therefore, I have selected examples of good witnesses in North Africa, both missionaries and nationals, to illustrate the caliber of the fine "soldiers of the Cross" who have given their lives in the service of God for the building of the Church there. They were willing to suffer and even die if that was God's will. But they were determined to live without compromise. The purpose of these illustrations is to show what the pressures and dangers are in a Muslim territory not only to the missionary visitor but especially to the national who, deciding for Christ, cuts himself off from family and friends and becomes, in the eyes of some, at least of his fellow citizens, a traitor to his people and country. As you will see, the form and degree of persecution varies from place to place and in different periods of time. But the threat is still there and the Christian must be armed by faith against it.

Dr. Leach: 1896

It was less than two months after their arrival in Sfax, Tunisia, that in the dark of night, thieves broke into the home of Dr. Charles Leach and murdered him, his wife and their six-year-old son, Charlie; somehow their 18-month-old daughter escaped.

It is instructive to contrast the experience of the Leaches with that of Miss Frances Banks. Miss Banks went out to Morocco in 1886 when she was 23 years old. She served in many different cities, principally in Casablanca, usually providing for her needs from private sources. After many years of faithful service she died in Tangier in 1954 aged 91. So the point is, whether in the will of God it be two months or 67 years, were you faithful in the place of God's appointment; did you keep on until your work was ended?

The Leach family had gone out from England to join an American working among Kabyles. Not long afterward this small Mission collapsed and after staying on for a few months alone, the Leaches joined NAM in 1891 and were posted to Tunis to start a medical work there. Somehow they felt strongly led to relocate further south in Sfax. Finally in March of 1896, they set up a medical work in their new location. Less than two months later they were dead. It was not until eleven years later that the station was reopened. That year Dr. and Mrs. Churcher moved to Sfax from Sousse.

There is a gravestone in Sfax recording the martyrdom of this young couple (36 years old) which contains their witness in the following words, "There is one God and one Mediator between God and man, the man Christ Jesus, Who gave Himself a ransom for all" (I Timothy 2:4). It is carved in French and Arabic for all to see. Three years after their martyrdom, Mr. Joseph Cooksey, paid a visit to the cemetery and later to the house itself, still unoccupied. There a guardian explained how the murderers had barred the door from the outside, climbed onto the roof, descended a small flight of stairs to the bedroom and killed the sleeping occupants. There was still a blood-stain visible on the floor.

The Leaches died in service; but not necessarily for their faith. It was simply part of living in a dangerous world.

Mr. David Cooper: 1900

When Miss Emma Herdman died there was need for someone
new to head up the program of training and directing the
activities of native colporteurs which she had started. The
Council felt that David Cooper would be the right person,
possibly, in part at least, since he too had come from Belfast in
Northern Ireland. So he left his post in Tripoli to travel via
London—to confer with the Council—to Tangier arriving in the
spring of 1900. October 2nd a party, including the Coopers and
their two small children, set out for the long trip by road to Fes.
Because of bad weather it took twelve days to cover the 165
miles. However, they all arrived safely on Monday the 13th.

Friday of that week at 11 A.M. Mr. Cooper and two
colporteurs went into the market to buy some matting. A man
rushed out of a nearby mosque and shot Mr. Cooper in the back.
After 2 and one-half hours of agony Mr. Cooper died, but not
before committing his wife and children to the Lord in prayer.
The murderer fled for refuge to the sacred Moulay Idris Mosque
where criminals normally find asylum. However, in this case,
when the Sultan heard about it, he had the man dragged from
the mosque and beaten with whips. Then he was draped across
a donkey and taken around the city as a warning. When the
Sultan learned that Mr. Cooper had died, he ordered that the
murderer be shot. The execution took place within an hour of
Mr. Cooper's death.

It was later discovered that the murderer was a so-called holy
man who had taken a vow to kill the first Nazrani (Christian) he
met. So he had come into town, sold some wheat in order to buy
a gun, and then went to the market square to look for a Nazrani.
When arrested he boasted of his act before the Sultan and
chided other Muslims for not doing the same. Many of the
country people sympathized with him in his devotion to Islam,
but most of the educated ones did not. And the Sultan opposed
such action strongly. He even went so far as to make a gift of
1000 pounds to the widow out of sympathy and promised a
military escort if she intended to travel homewards.

The attack was neither instigated nor accepted by the
government. It was the act of a fanatic. I do not know of a
missionary who was executed for his faith by the government.

They have been arrested often; jailed occasionally, and expelled frequently; but never executed. Treatment of nationals who become Christians is another thing. They often suffer bitterly even to the death. Perhaps action against converts is not as severe today as it once was. But it is often difficult to find out what happened when a known Christian disappears.

Dr. and Mrs. Campbell: 1974

After serving for many years in TMH at Tangier, Bill Campbell moved south to Safi and set up in private practice. In addition, he and his wife, Holly, shepherded the little group of Christians in Safi and were widely known for their religious convictions.

A cassette tape they were sending home to a relative was intercepted by the postal authorities. When they audited it, they heard messages and songs from both missionaries and nationals. This apparently triggered an investigation. All known Christians were called in for interrogation. Finally, the Campbells were arrested and remanded for trial.

The initial charge was that they were evangelizing. But Bill, reading from the Moroccan Constitution, claimed that he was only "practising his religion," a right guaranteed all citizens. So the charges were changed and they were accused of using bribes in order to persuade Muslims to abandon their religion; that is, indeed, prohibited by law.

Oddly enough, the testimony in support of these charges was cited from Moroccans who were no longer in the country and therefore could not be cross-examined. On the other hand, several Moroccan Christians present sought permission to testify in behalf of the Campbells, but were not permitted to do so. Muslim authorities felt things had gotten out of hand. Instead of intimidating the missionaries, and especially the national Christians, and shaming the Christian cause, the reverse had taken place. Christians, foreign and Moroccan, were found to be calmly fearless and willing at any risk to stand by their convictions. This had to be stopped. So one day soon afterward, plain clothes policemen assembled the Campbell family and escorted them out of the country.

The Campbell story is a good illustration of persecution for a clear uncompromising witness. They were arrested, interrogated, jailed briefly, accused falsely, condemned and expelled. But they never wavered. And, together with about a dozen other members of NAM, having been put out of one country they have gone back into another in order to continue their witness. They are certainly good martyrs in the sense of the Greek work, if not according to the popular concept.

Si Ali: 1944

Mrs. Simpson, of Guercif, who arrived in England from Morocco in January, 1945, received news on Christmas Eve of the homecall of her faithful native Christian fellow-laborer in the Gospel, Si Ali. He had succumbed to mercurial poisoning. This is how Mrs. Simpson writes about it.

A letter from Si Ali's eldest son, dated December 10 and received this morning says; "Father has gone to God." There were no details—not even the date of his death.

Since his second poisoning, 18 months ago, and by a neighboring tribe (*not* his own folk, most of whom had grown to respect and even love him, in spite of his "infidelity"), I have felt that he could not come through, as was the case in 1906 when Dr. Vardon said "the amount of mercury administered actually saved him, as it could not be retained." But that meant years of suffering, and nursing sympathy.

The poison given in April 1943 has entailed even greater suffering, though development was slower.

It matters little concerning his mortal remains . . . For years he has been threatened with non-burial— to be thrown on a rubbish heap to be eaten by dogs. He has gone to his Heavenly home with wondrously filled hands. Would that each of us might be similarly honored. ". . . With what joy my dear husband will have greeted his child in the faith of 1903!"

How we praise God for this moving story of a loyal, simple-hearted Moroccan who was "faithful unto death."

El-Kaid: 1902

Few of the missionaries knew his family name, so
they referred to him as El-Kaid or the Captain;
because when he first came for religious instruction,
he was an officer in the local battery of artillery.
Twelve years ago he was won to Christ through
reading the Scriptures in our Tangier Depot. Since
then, notwithstanding "persecutions oft" besides
the common difficulties and temptations of life, he
has maintained his faith in the Lord Jesus Christ. He
bears the honor of being one of the Gospel first-fruits
in Morocco.

The missionaries with whom El-Kaid had dealings
in the course of his Bible work testified to his sterling
Christian character, his eager appreciation of spiritual truth, and his diligence in service. His zeal led
him into difficult situations. Once, in Larache, a
fanatical Moslem, standing on one of the highest
shrines of the town, denounced him as a renegade
and infidel, and called upon the townsmen to put him
to death. From that time he became a marked man,
and a band of violent fanatics attacked him in the
open street and maltreated him so severely that he
succumbed to the injuries then received. His old
mother tells that during his last hours, and even
while he lay in delirium, his relatives did their
utmost to persuade him to testify to the apostleship
of Muhammad and so die as a Moslem, but that in
reply to all their entreaties "he only spoke of Jesus."

(Mr. William Summers in
The Bible Society Reporter)

Mustafa Jabiri; 1975

The case of Mustafa Jabiri serves to point up the fact that
the same man with identical witness and lifestyle will be treated
differently under different circumstances.

Mustafa was brought up in the town of Demnat in the hills of
Morocco. The population of Demnat is almost evenly divided
between Muslims and Jews but most are of Berber stock. As a
young man, Mustafa moved to Casablanca, trained in radio

communications and got a job at the International Airport. Incidentally, his boss at the airport, Abdel Latif, was an old friend and neighbor from Demnat; also a Berber.

Later on, Mustafa passed through an agonizing period when he was deeply convicted of his sins and eventually became a Christian. He led his wife to Christ and they brought up their children as Christians. In fact, as a leader in the local assembly, Mustafa was well-known throughout Casablanca as a Christian.

Years later he went home to Demnat for a visit. It was during the month of Ramadan when Muslims fast all day long and therefore are angry when they see anyone break the fast by eating. Of course, as a Christian, Mustafa ate during the day. He was seen to do so and accused as a law-breaker to the authorities. In spite of his testimony that he was a Christian, Mustafa was adjudged guilty and was sentenced to prison for six months.

His family took refuge with his Muslim parents and Christian friends made generous gifts of money and food for them while he was in prison. Of course, he lost his job because of his crime. But the amazing thing is that when Mustafa was released, his boss and all seventeen of his associates at work, all Muslims, signed a petition directed to the Government disciplinary committee requesting that Mustafa be restored to his job. They all knew he was a Christian but that did not matter. They respected him as a man of character and appreciated his work. So he is working again at the airport and, as a Christian, refusing to observe the Muslim month of fasting. He did not die. He was imprisoned. But he did not compromise his Christian convictions.

Rahma

Rahma became acquainted with missionaries in Relizane, Algeria when she was a young girl. Her family were Muslims. But her father valued the training she got at the mission house because there were not schools for girls at the time. He tolerated the religion that was also taught there. This happy situation went on for several years until the father died. Now the oldest son took control of the household. He hated Christians and was ashamed that his sister claimed to be one, so he forbade her to go to the missionaries any more. As time went on his suspicion grew that his sister was, in fact, seeing the missionaries anyway in spite of his orders—otherwise how could she remain so cheerful and continue singing those hated songs. So he locked her in a dark, back room of the house. She was allowed out only to work; and the hardest and dirtiest tasks were heaped upon her. After a time, overworked and underfed, she succumbed to T.B. and gradually became weaker and weaker until she had not strength to leave her dark prison. Only her mother would come to visit her.

One day when her mother was with her in the room she seemed to gain strength from some unknown source, sat up on her mat and said, "Mother, visitors are coming, please prepare coffee for them." (This is the normal act of hospitality.)

"Oh, no, dear," said her mother, "no one is allowed to come back here."

"Yes," replied Rahma, "I can see them. They have come to take me home." With that she fell back on the mat and ceased breathing. A martyr? Yes, though almost completely unknown to people outside. She refused to compromise or complain; she suffered and died.

Good witnesses sometimes become martyrs, by popular definition. All Christians who die in service do not necessarily qualify as martyrs. But the distinction is more attractive than significant.

A Moroccan girl, for example, who becomes a Christian before marriage with a clear testimony to a sound knowledge of the truth and walk with the Lord, then is shut up by her husband from any further contact or fellowship with other Christians for the rest of her life, yet maintains a joyful witness to the Lord is, in my opinion, a jewel of great price to God whether martyr or not. So likewise a man who becomes a Christian after marriage and for his consistent Christian walk is despised by his Muslim wife and children, hounded by relatives and friends, finds employment difficult and jobs scarce, yet maintains a sweet testimony to the Lord, is a gem in the diadem of the King.

Doubtless many thousands of such precious souls have been won to Christ over the many years of Gospel witness to North

Africa. And though unknown to men, are precious to God. Because of the forced obscurity of their lives they are not the kind of Christians who will become foundation stones in the new Church in North Africa. And although we do not encourage secret believers who are such out of a feeble faith and fear, we honor those who maintained an indomitable faith under extreme circumstances.

Many a time the body of a known Christian has at death been taken from home and family to be buried by Muslim relatives in a Muslim grave with great show and ostentation in an effort to erase the despised testimony of the deceased. But at the resurrection many Christians will rise from Muslim graves refuting this false appearance and join the Lord of Glory in the skies.

As the national Church grows in North Africa it will give refuge to many presently fearful believers and increasingly witness to the greater power of Him that is with us than him that is in the world. For this we need to pray for those who will not count their souls as dear unto death, but will witness a good confession even if need be on occasion sealed by their life's blood.

FUTURE PROSPECTS

It seems almost foolhardy to speculate about the future of the NAM, the work of God in North Africa or, perhaps most important of all, the North African Church. Following the Muslim invasion which hastened the destruction and disappearance of the national church in North Africa there was a long period when there appeared no hope at all for the rebirth of that once vigorous, glorious Church. The early years of missionary work saw a slowly increasing growth of Christian witness. Many, perhaps thousands of individual converts, were won from Islam by painful efforts. European political tensions affected the conduct of missionary work almost as much as national Islamic resistance.

Following World War I, with the downfall of the Ottoman Empire and the spread of European political control over formerly Muslim governments, a false optimism sprang up in certain Christian circles; now, more than ever before, it was thought, there will be opportunities for Christian nations to take advantage of the weakened Muslim authorities and press the attack for the advance of the Gospel. But it just did not happen that way. In the first place the so-called Christian nations behaved in a most unChristian manner. In order to insure the economic exploitation of their new charges, treaties were often drafted prohibiting the spread of the Gospel so as not to annoy the natives.

Then, too, there was a renascence of Islam in several of its different branches as diverse as Ahmaddiyya in India (and later Pakistan) and Wahabi in Saudi Arabia which served to strengthen Muslim resistance to Christianity. On top of this the shameful neglect of Muslim peoples by churches and missionary societies only aggravated an already dismal situation. Then as interest in and concern for the Muslim world began to grow in the Christian west, seeds of nationalism sown years before began to sprout with renewed vigor by the close of World War II and new obstacles confronted the missionary endeavor.

But now that the necessary adjustments to the new situation in North Africa have been made and the goal of a national church has been brought more clearly into focus so that these churches are finally making their appearance, what are the prospects for further church growth and what part will expatriate missionaries have in that development? Perhaps we should start by reminding ourselves of one supreme fact; the future of the Gospel ministry and church growth in North Africa depends on the plan God has for North Africa and our involvement in that plan by His direction and power.

Certain practical questions, however, bear upon the problem. How will the Western nations handle the energy crisis? How healthy will their economic growth be? What chance is there of a devastating war world-wide or economic crisis? And to what degree will Christians in the Western countries be able to avoid the distraction of world events and maintain biblical priorities even if at some considerable sacrifice to personal desires and comforts? Or, perhaps we should ask; will it be Third World Christians who assist in the growth of the North African Church rather than those from the "decadent" West?

I suppose the best answer is not just to guess and hope but

believe and act. The future then will be as bright as our
obedient faith in the plan of God can make it. In any case, as we
confront the future we do so with profound gratitude to the
faithfulness of God over the past one hundred years. We are
challenged by the dedication and sacrifice of those of our family
who have preceded us. And we accept the encouraging exhorta-
tion of the Apostle Paul, "Therefore, my beloved brethren, be
ye steadfast, unmoveable, always abounding in the work of the
Lord, forasmuch as ye know that your labor is *not in vain* in the
Lord" I Corinthians 15:58.

INTERPRETING THE NUMBERS
[An Explanation of the Graph]

In considering the number of missionaries in the NAM at any period we must bear in mind that our basic mandate is the establishing of a truly independent church of converted Muslims in North Africa. Therefore the significant number of workers are those engaged in that program.

In order, therefore, to appreciate the true meaning of the statistics displayed by the graph we have to reckon with some qualifying factors. All of the personnel listed year by year were not primarily engaged in the central program. For example, before 1950 perhaps as many as a third of the total were engaged in work with Europeans.

Furthermore, for the last ten to fifteen years roughly forty percent of the total field force, not counting administrative personnel, were resident in France, not North Africa. Nevertheless, approximately twenty-five of them work in the Radio School of the Bible which, although not involved in direct personal contact with North Africans, is the indispensable first phase of evangelism which stirs interest and develops contact for the missionaries in North Africa.

Of far greater importance, however, is the fact that within the last ten years more and more of our people in North Africa have had to secure employment as Special Service Workers in order to obtain resident permits from the North African authorities. Their employment consumes a great deal of the working day, therefore reducing the time spent in direct ministry.

The inescapable conclusion to which these facts bring us is the need for many more skilled, dedicated people to work at the RSB and with Muslims in North Africa. We must find new methods for pioneers and partners to stimulate, then capitalize on the response to the Gospel. We must concentrate on present areas of response all the while seeking to generate new contacts so that the national Church will spring to life again and flourish in "the land of the vanished Church."

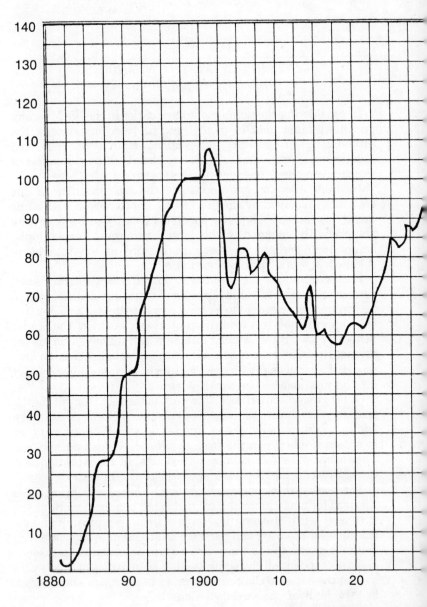

NUMBER OF FIEL

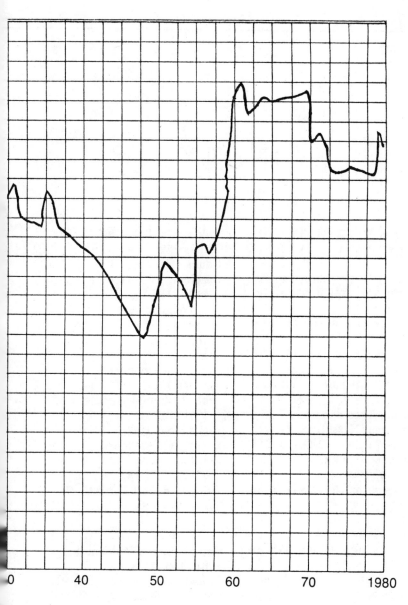

0   40   50   60   70   1980

MISSIONARIES PER YEAR

INDEX

About the Author

Francis R. Steele, Associate U.S. Director of North Africa Mission, has traveled extensively in Tunisia, Algeria, Morocco, and western Europe in his desire to communicate the spiritual needs of the Muslim world. Formerly Assistant Professor of Assyriology at the University of Pennsylvania and Assistant Curator of the Babylonian Section of the University Museum, Dr. Steele is a graduate of Cornell University and the University of Pennsylvania. He has served with NAM since 1953.